5	WE ROCK
12	PLAY MY MUSIC
19	GOTTA FIND YOU
25	START THE PARTY
32	WHO WILL I BE
38	THIS IS ME
45	HASTA LA VISTA
50	HERE I AM
55	TOO COOL
61	OUR TIME IS HERE
68	2 STARS
73	WHAT IT TAKES

Disney characters and artwork © Disney Enterprises, Inc.

ISBN 978-1-4234-6603-1

WALT DISNEY MUSIC COMPANY
WONDERLAND MUSIC COMPANY, INC.

DISTRIBUTED BY

7777 W. BLUEMOUND RD. P.O. BOX 13819 MILWAUKEE, WI 53213

In Australia Contact:
Hal Leonard Australia Pty. Ltd.
4 Lentara Court
Cheltenham, Victoria, 3192 Australia
Email: ausadmin@halleonard.com.au

For all works contained herein:
Unauthorized copying, arranging, adapting, recording or public performance is an infringement of copyright.
Infringers are liable under the law.

Visit Hal Leonard Online at
www.halleonard.com

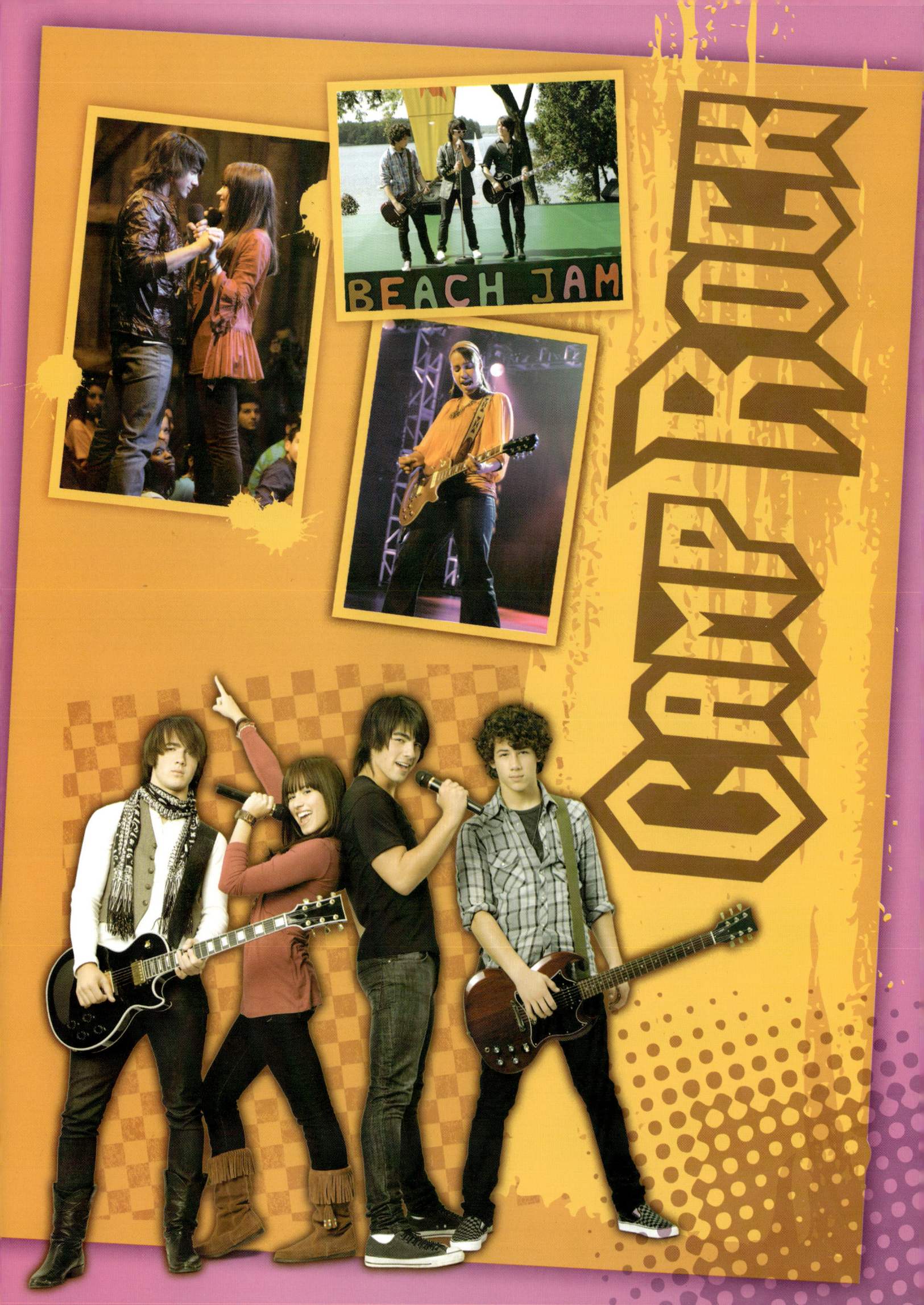

WE ROCK

Words and Music by KARA DioGUARDI and GREG WELLS

© 2008 Wonderland Music Company, Inc.
All Rights Reserved Used by Permission

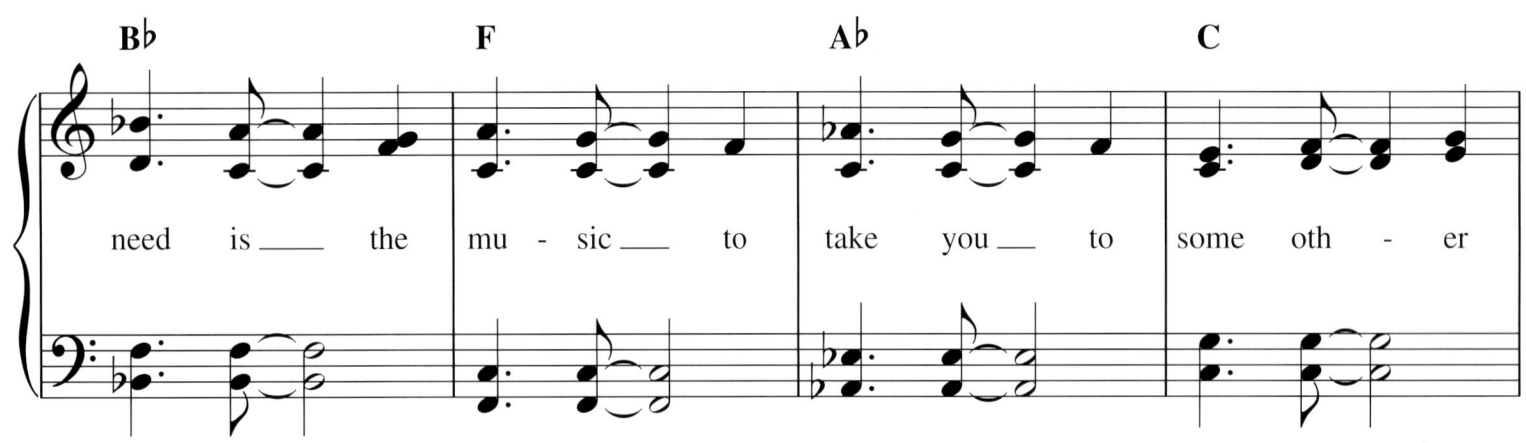
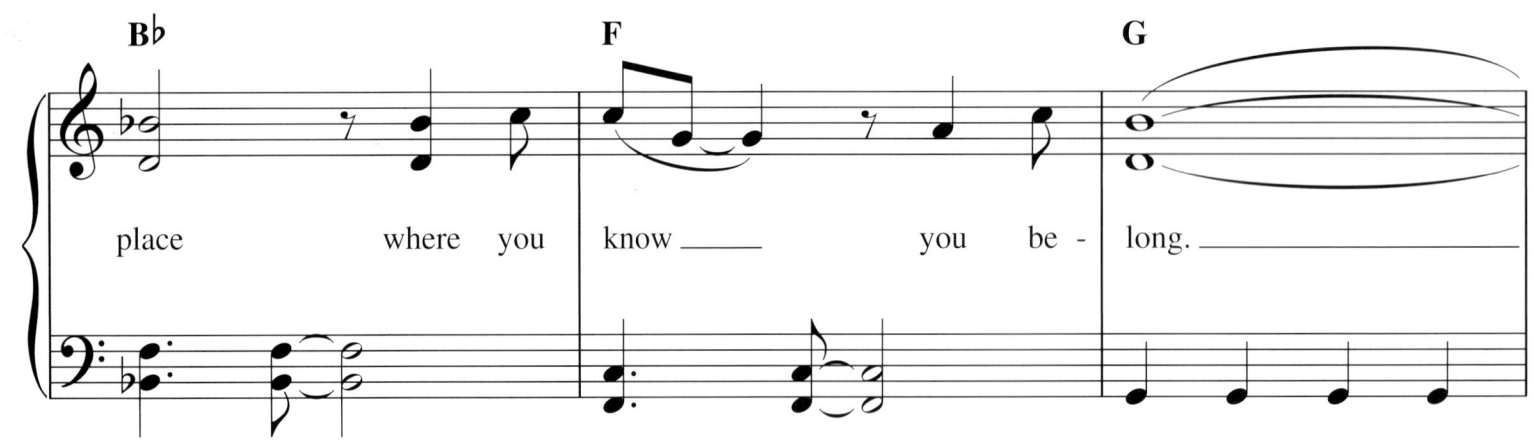

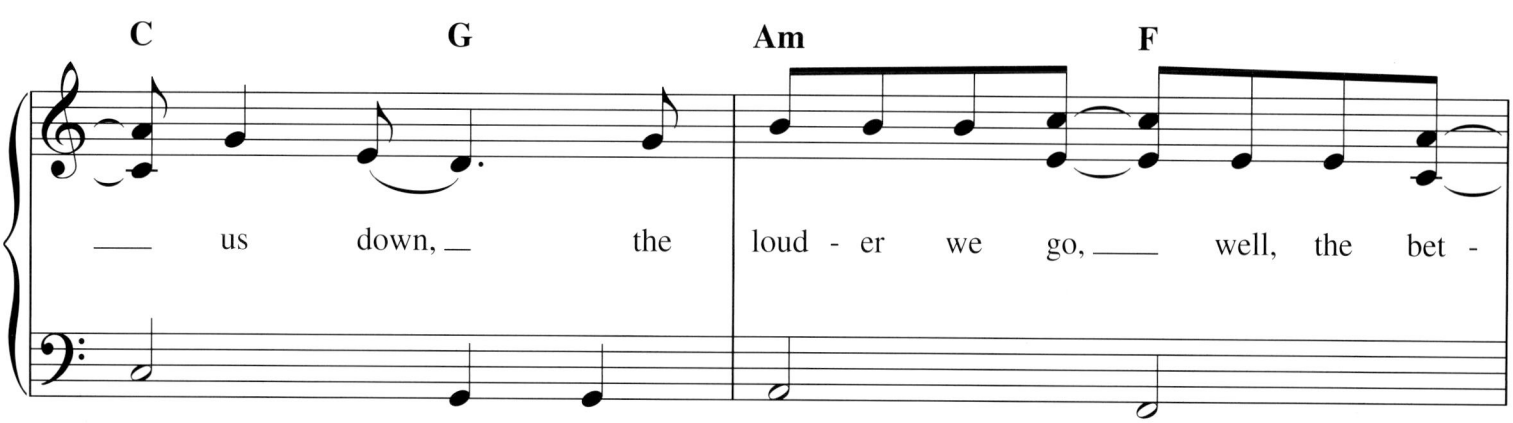

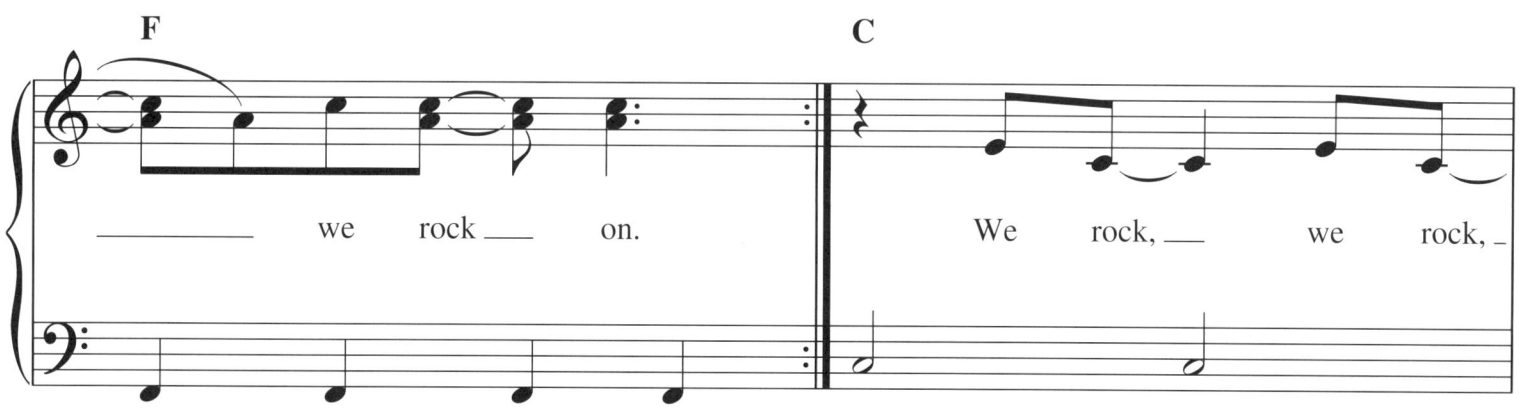

PLAY MY MUSIC

Words and Music by KARA DioGUARDI
and MITCH ALLAN

© 2008 Wonderland Music Company, Inc. and Walt Disney Music Company
All Rights Reserved   Used by Permission

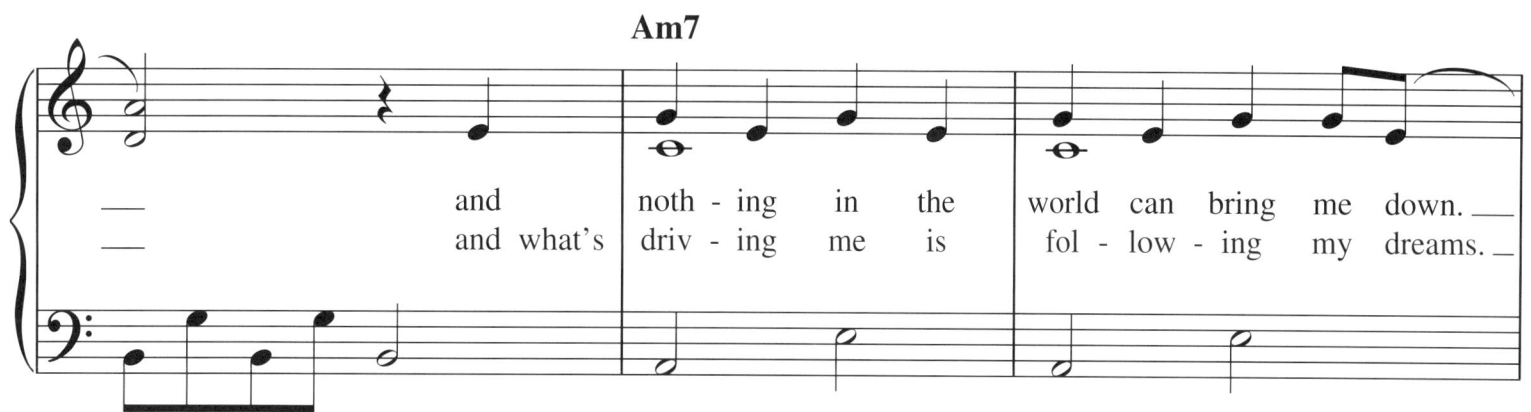

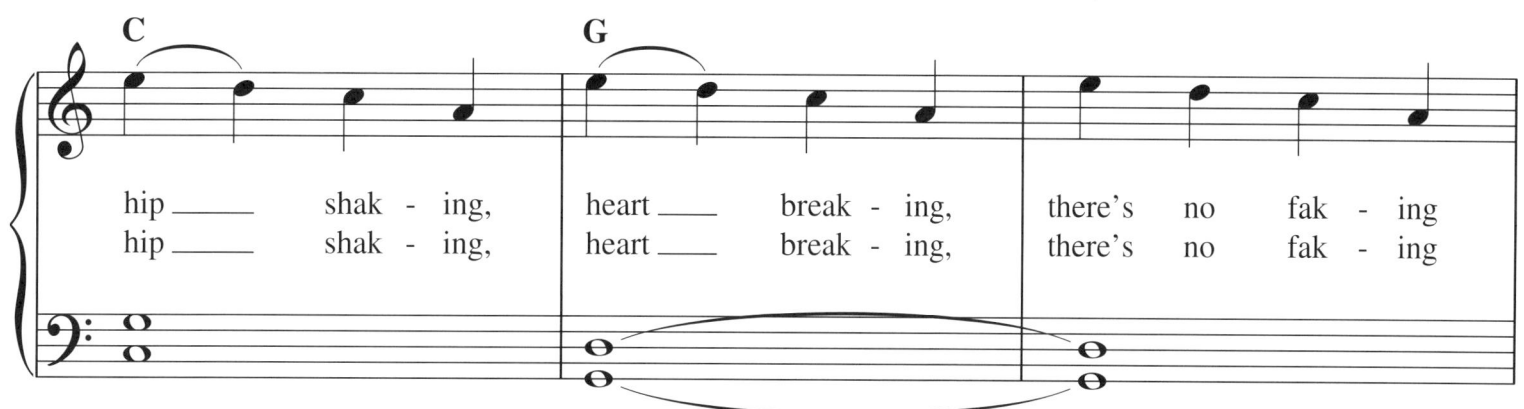

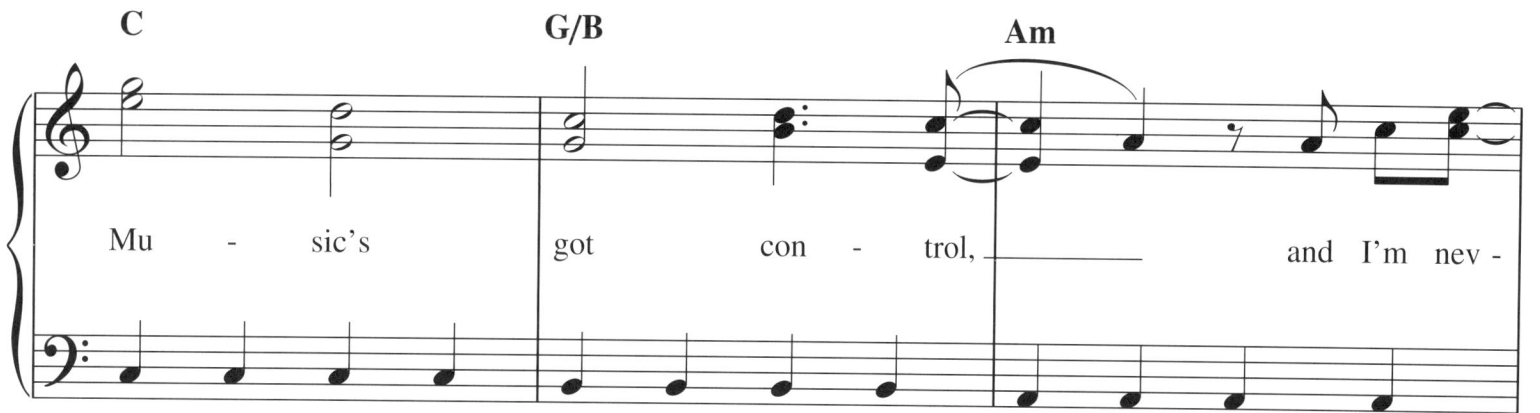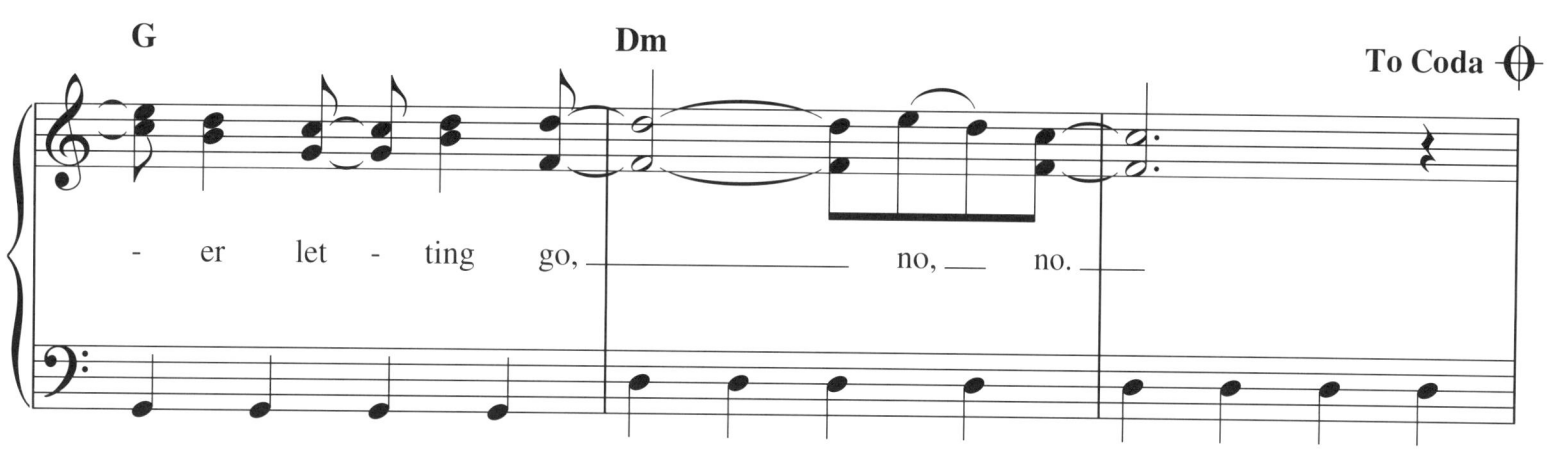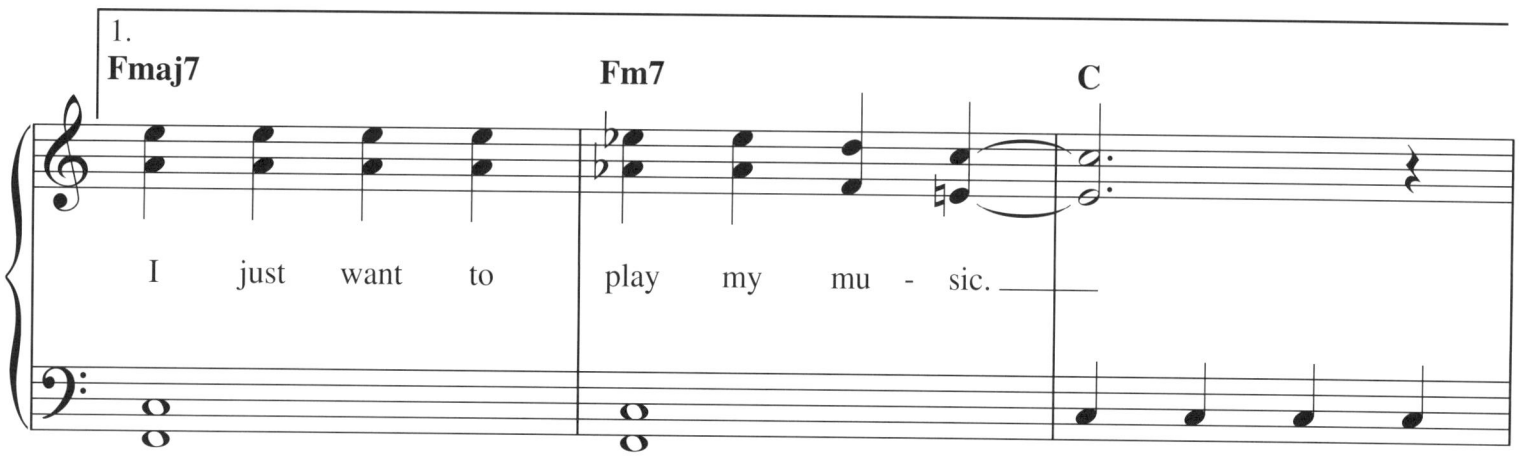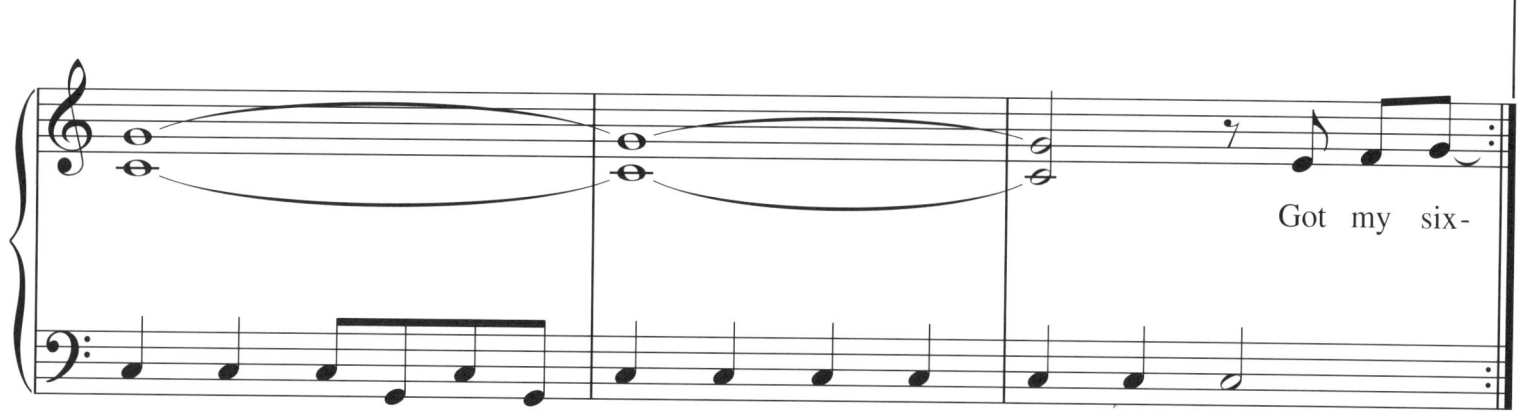

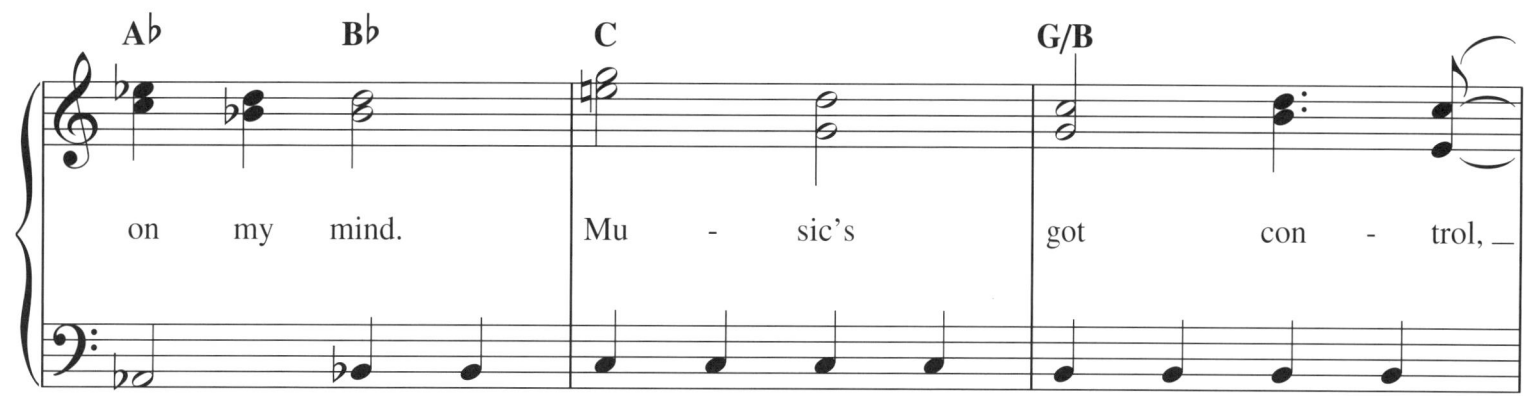

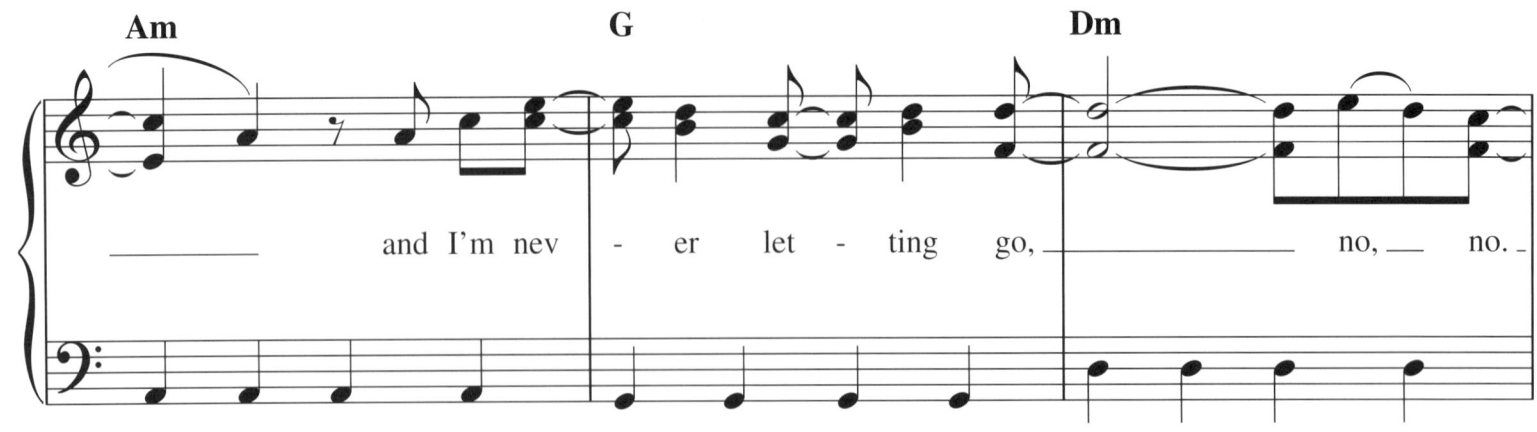

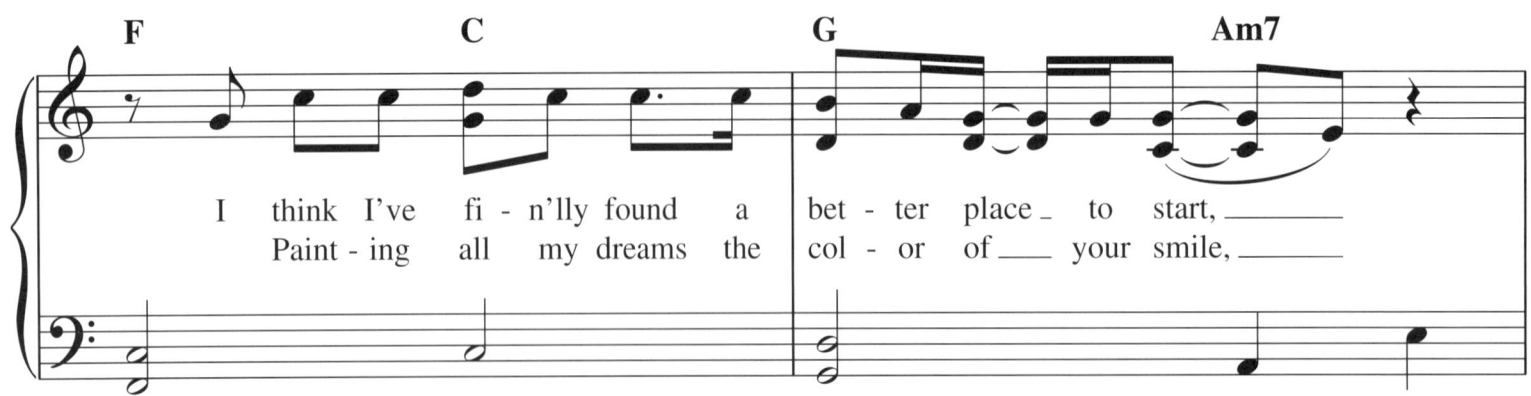
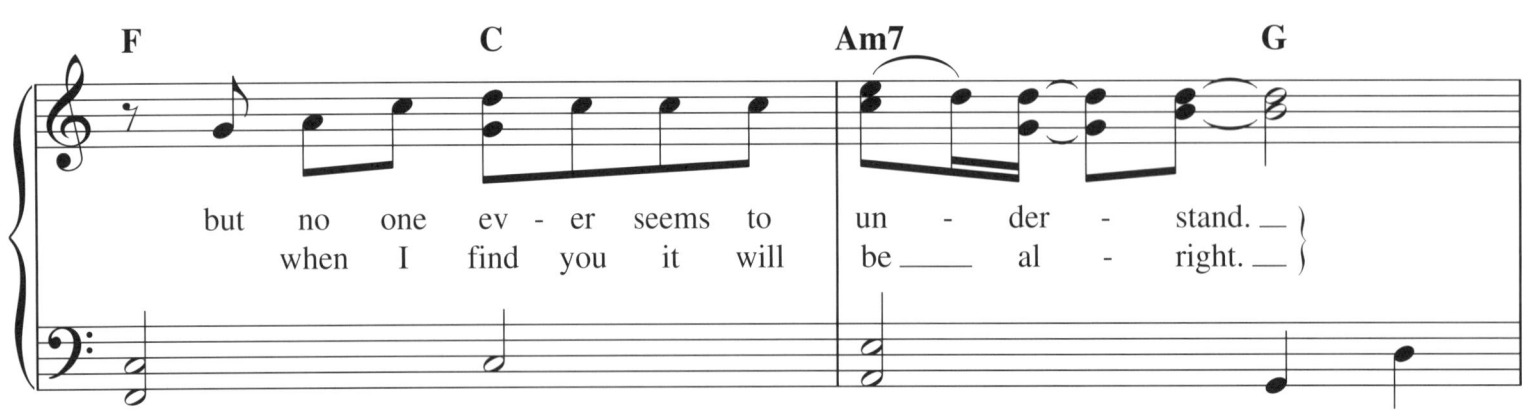

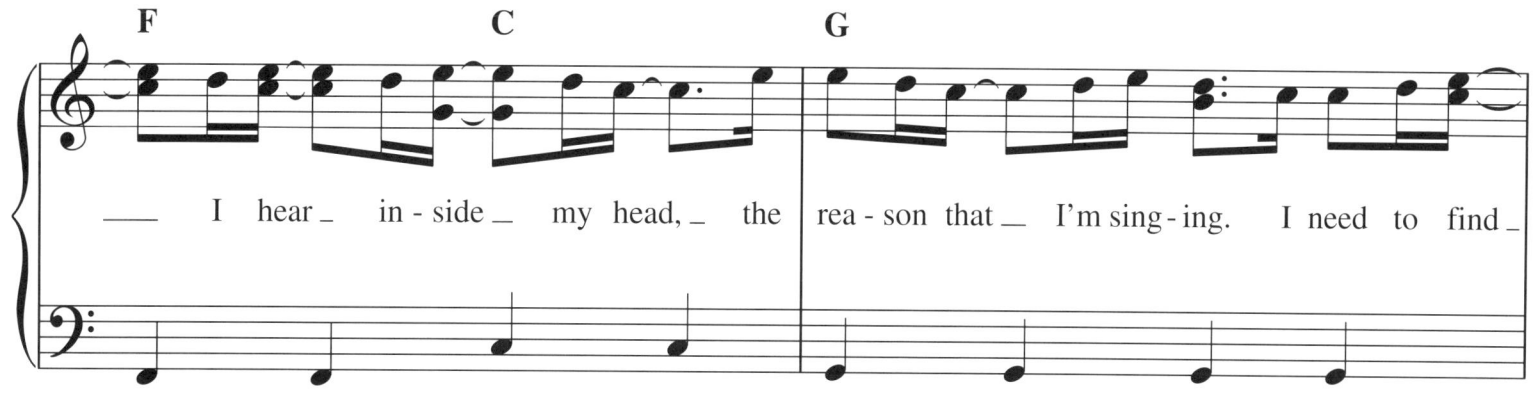

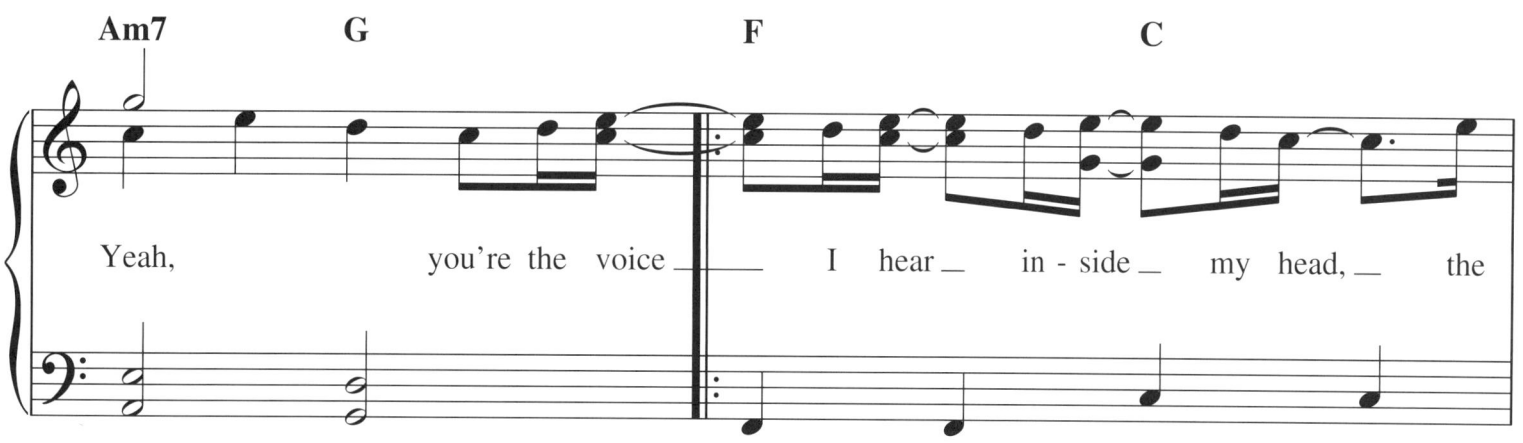

START THE PARTY

Words and Music by MATTHEW GERRARD
and ROBBIE NEVIL

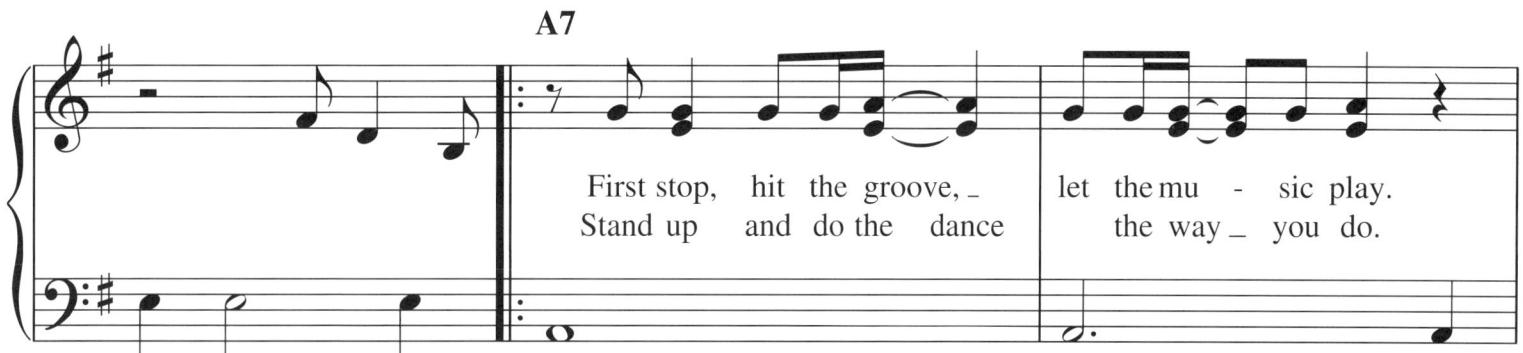
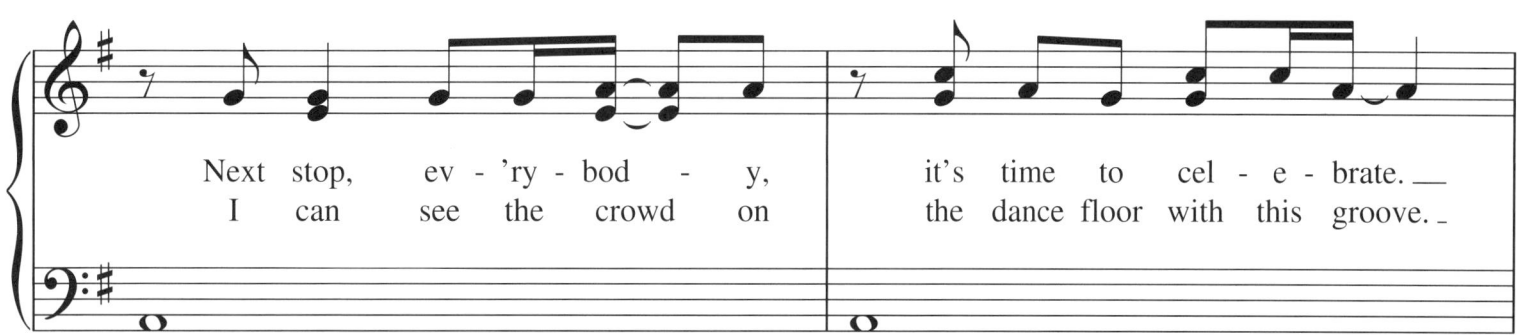

© 2008 Walt Disney Music Company
All Rights Reserved Used by Permission

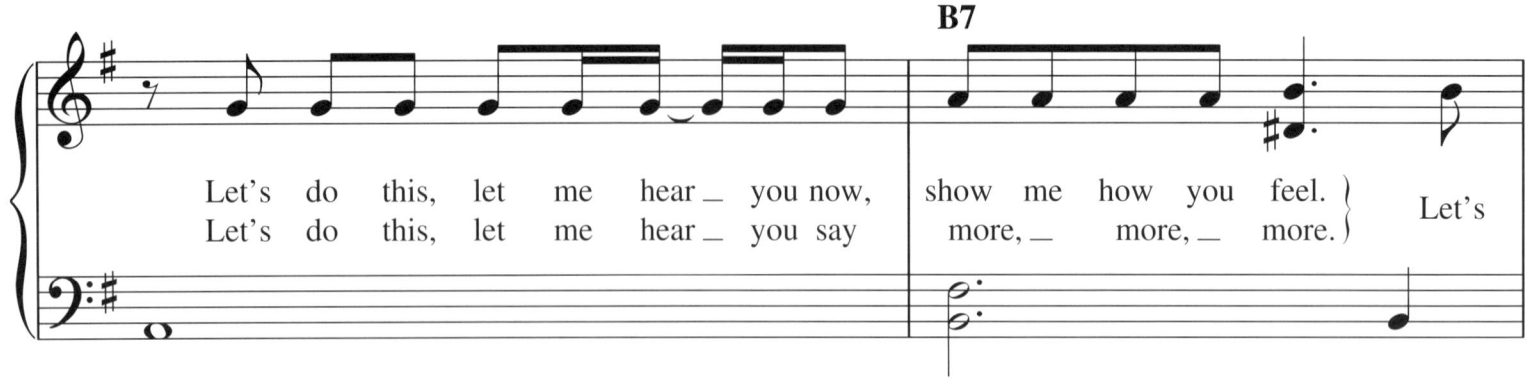
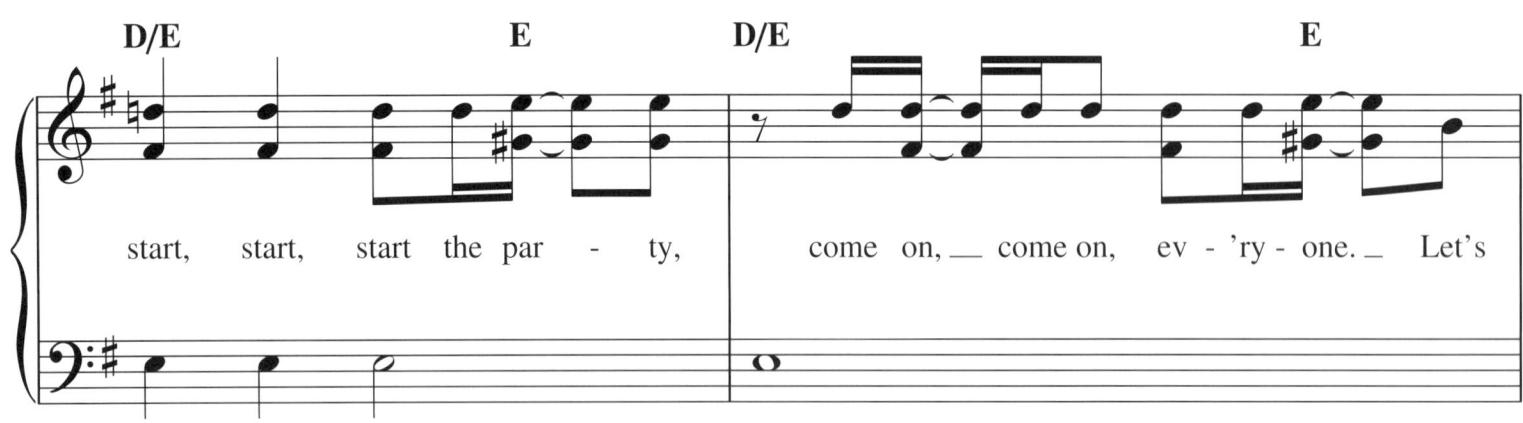
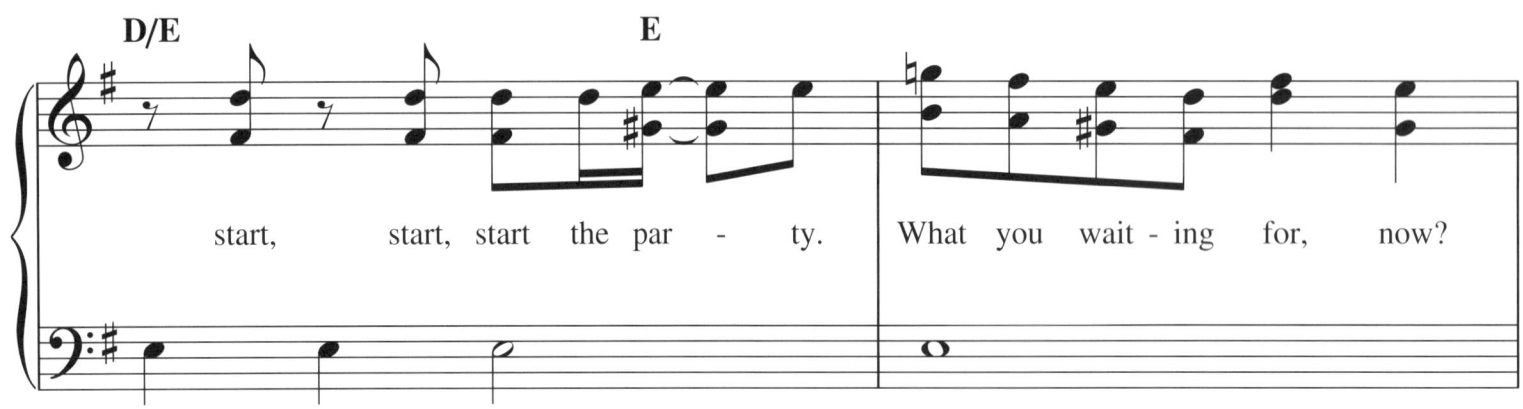
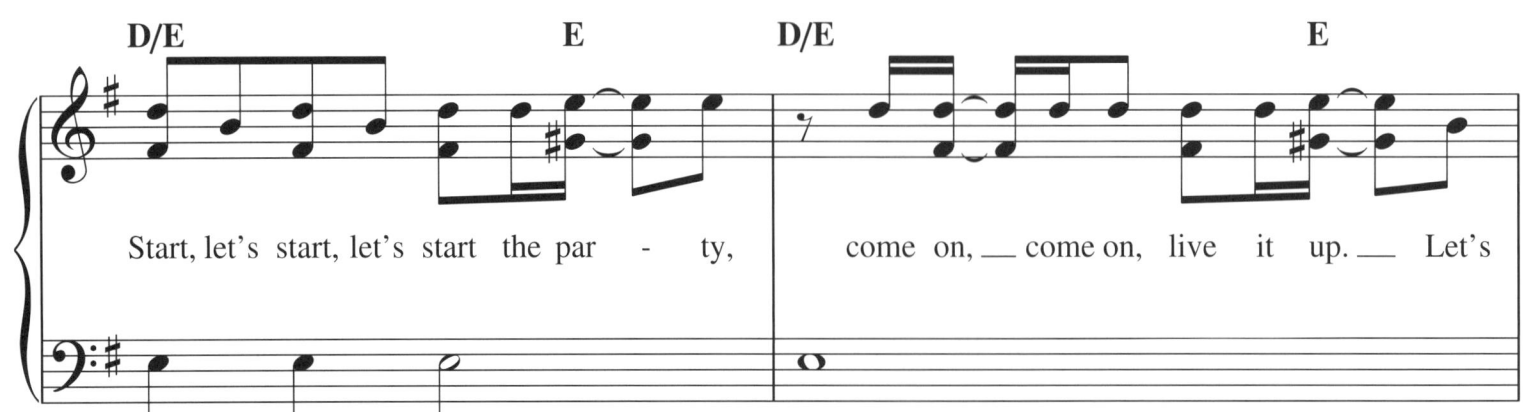

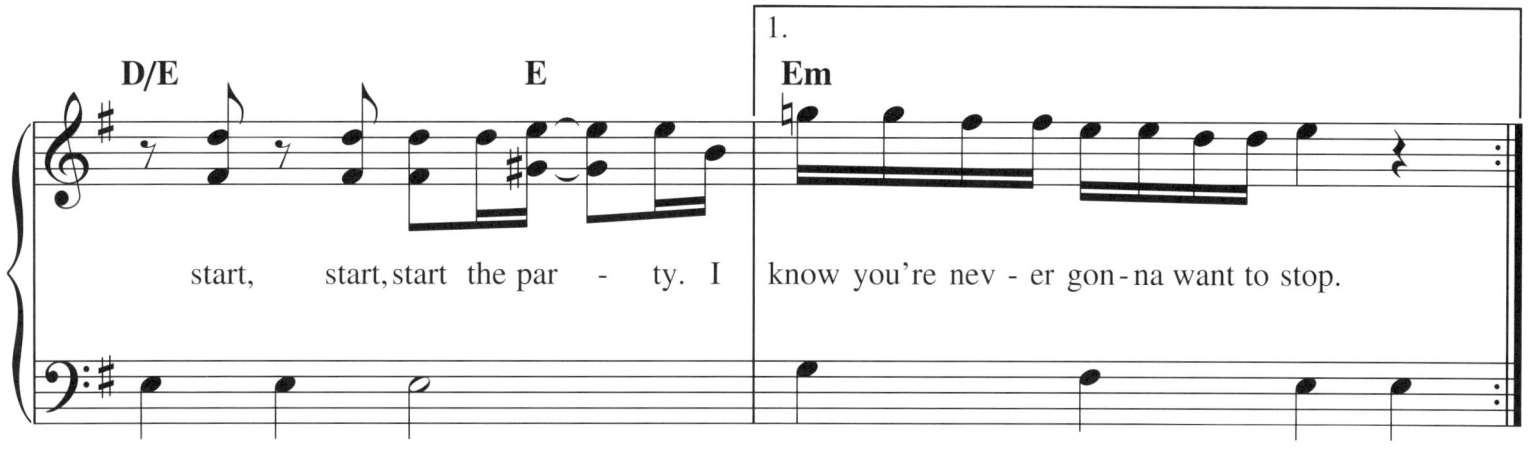

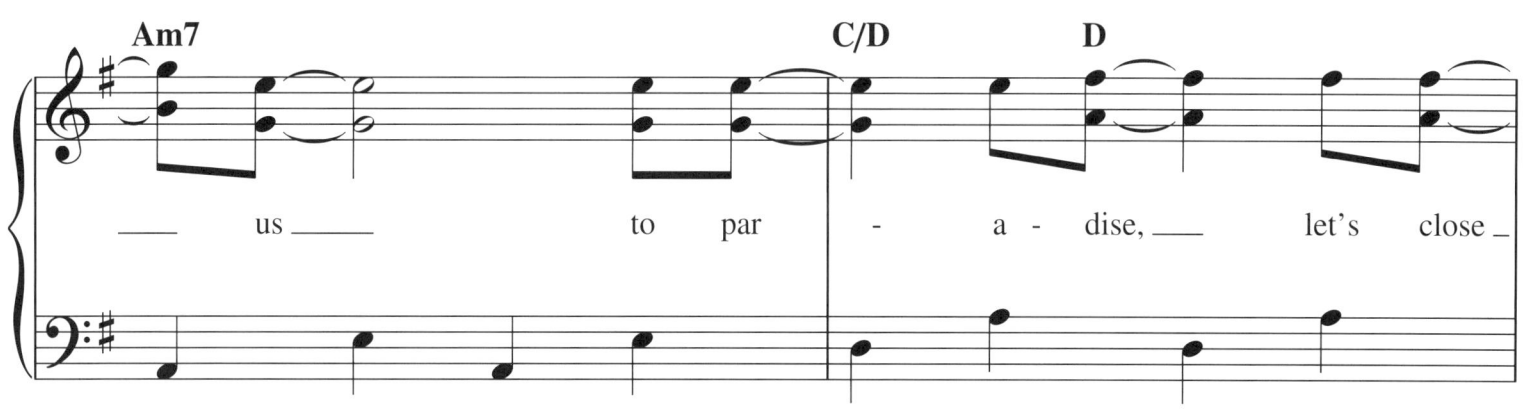
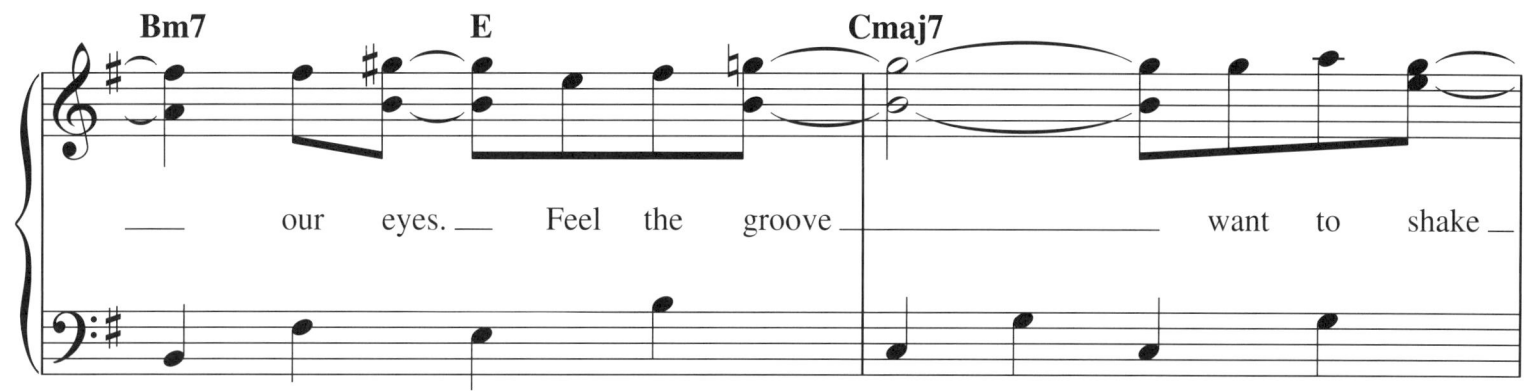

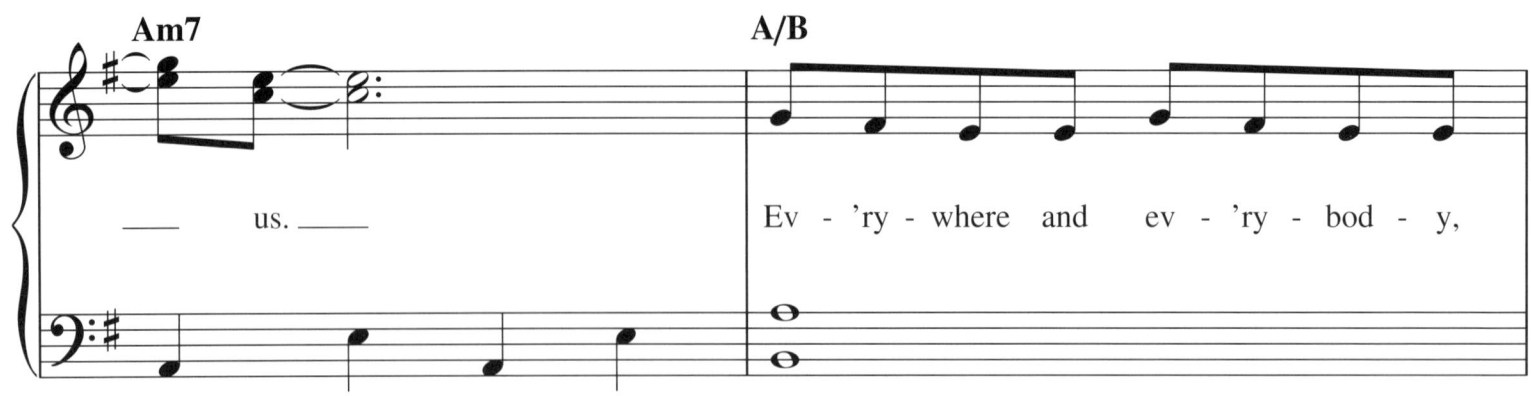
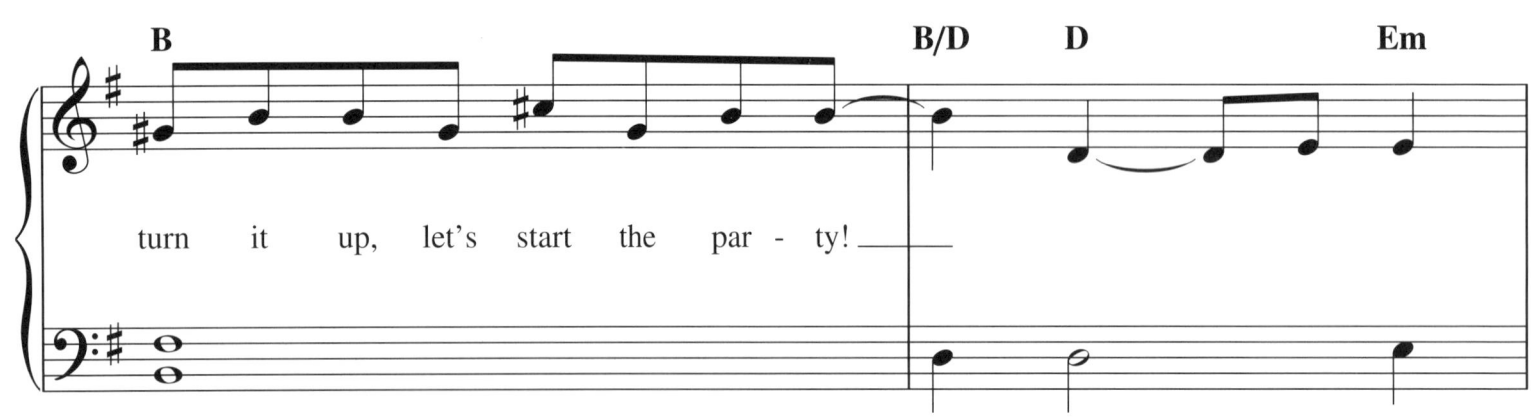

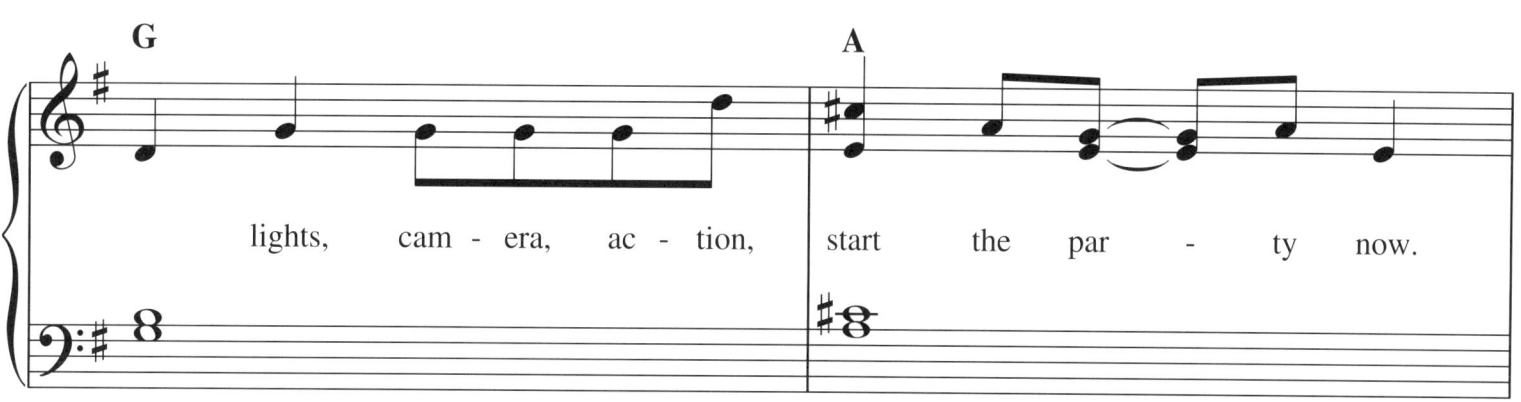
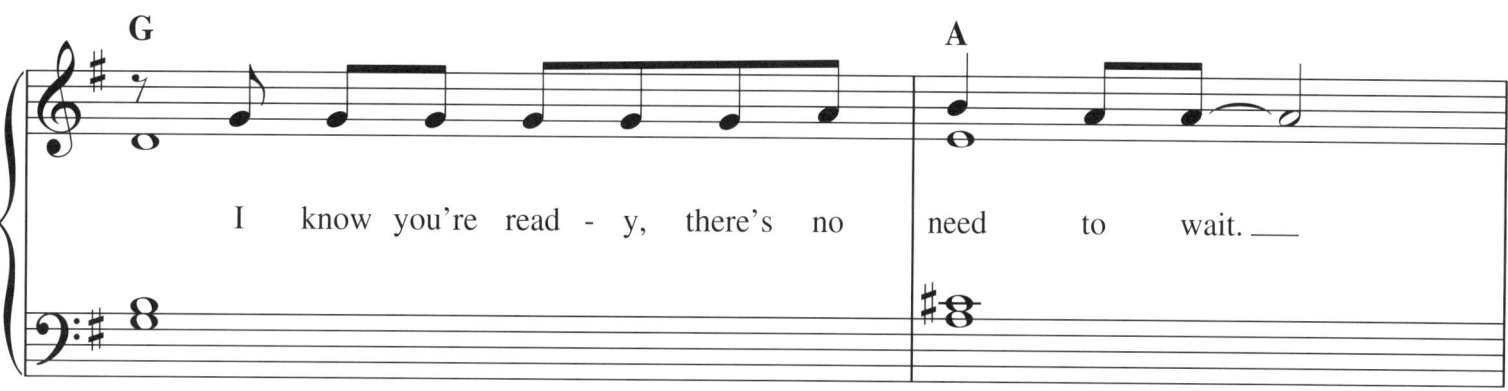
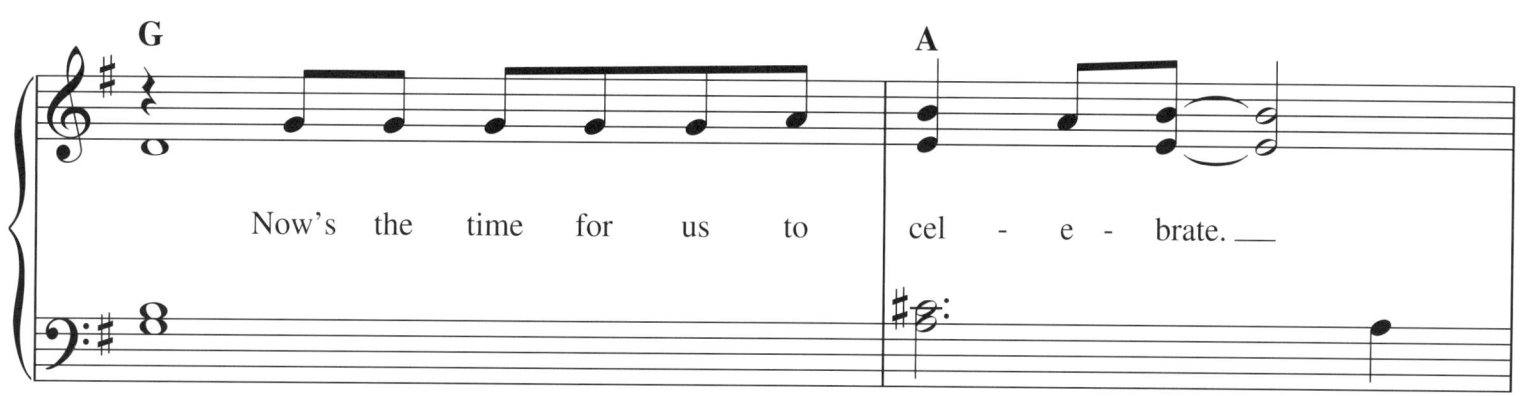

B
Em
(Spoken:) Start, start the party,
let's do it.
Start, start the party,
everybody now.
Start, start the party,
let's get to it.
Start, start the party.
D/E
E
D/E
E
Start, start, start the par - ty,
come on, come on, ev - 'ry- one. Let's

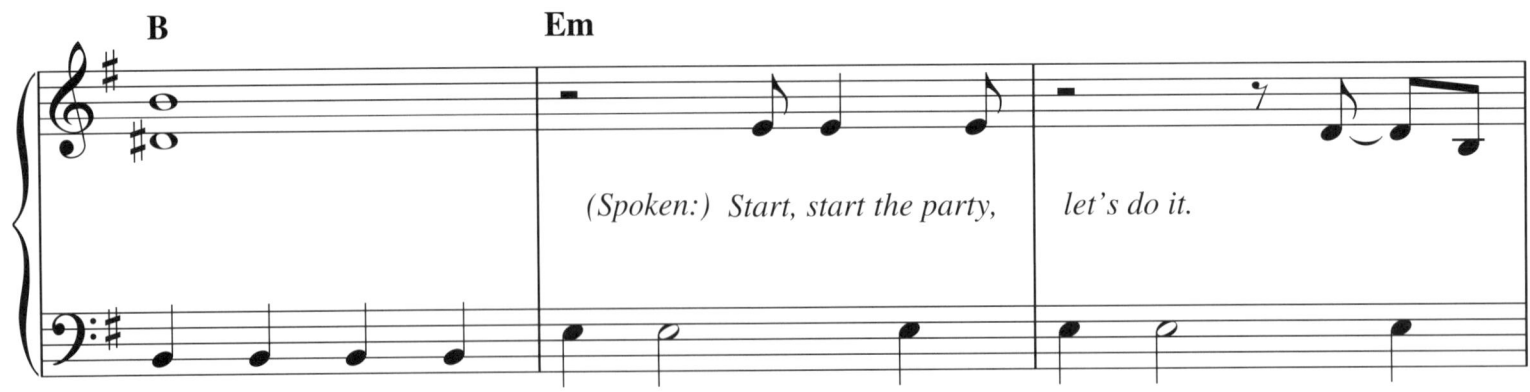

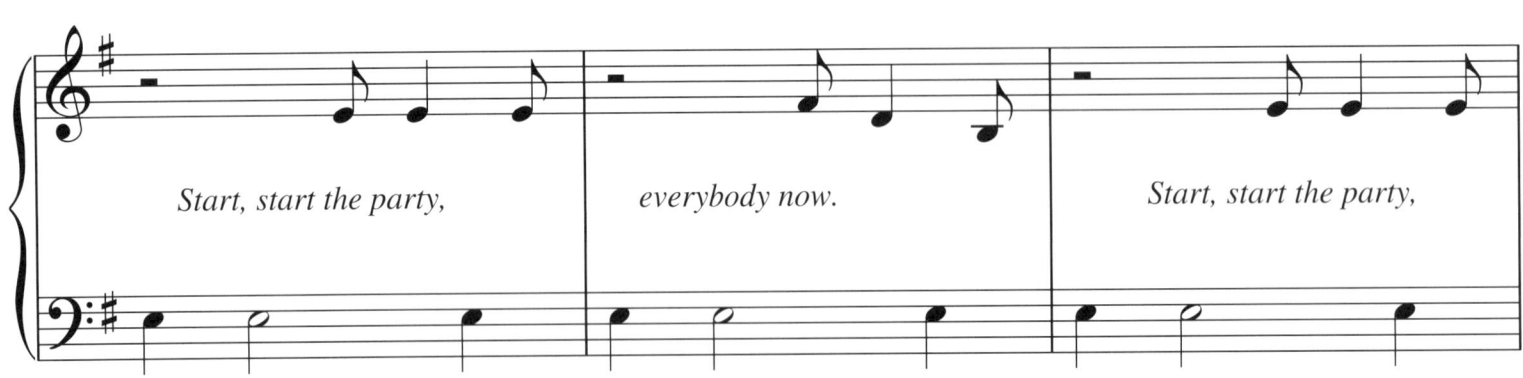

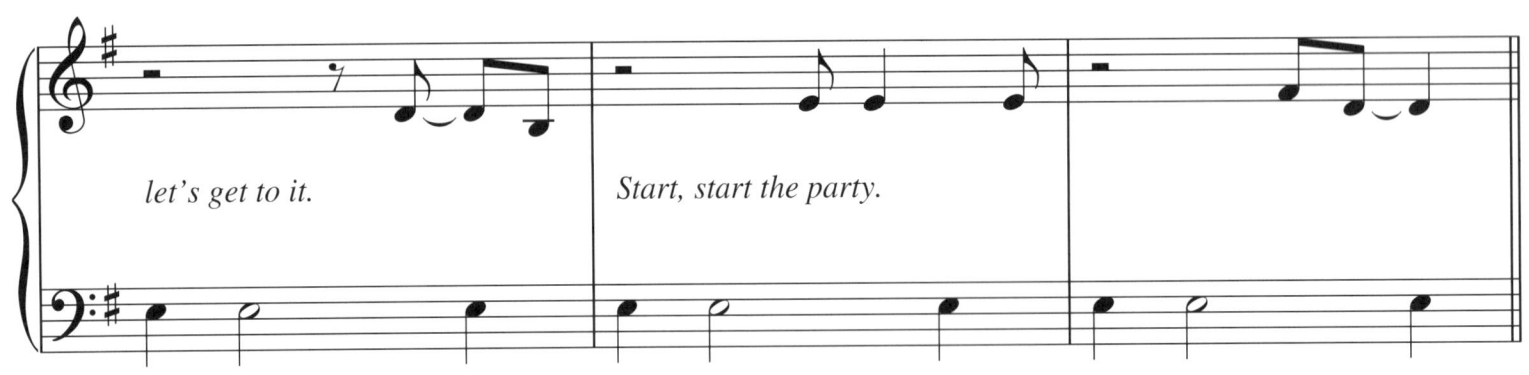

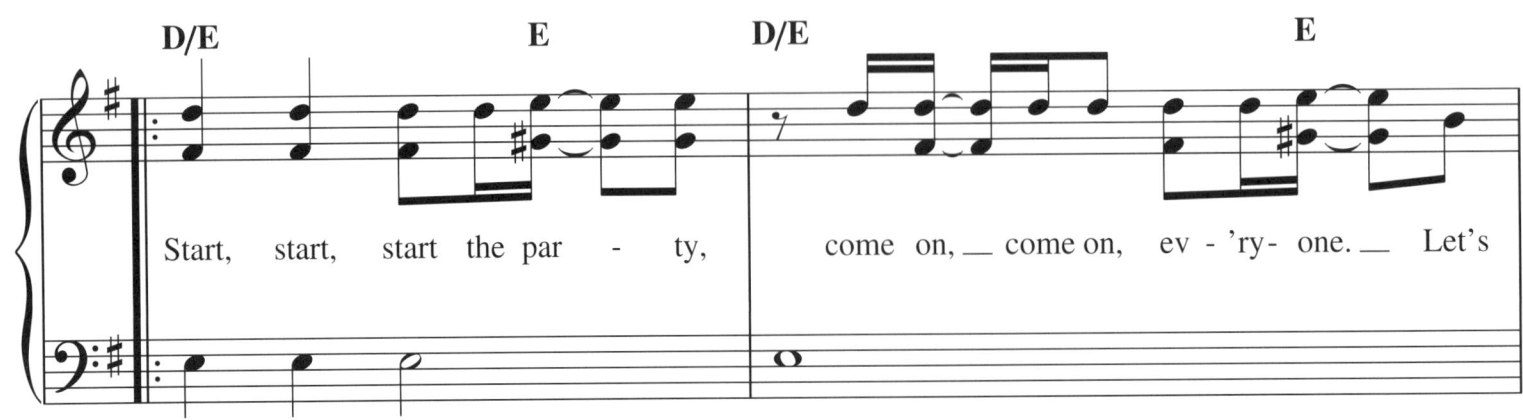

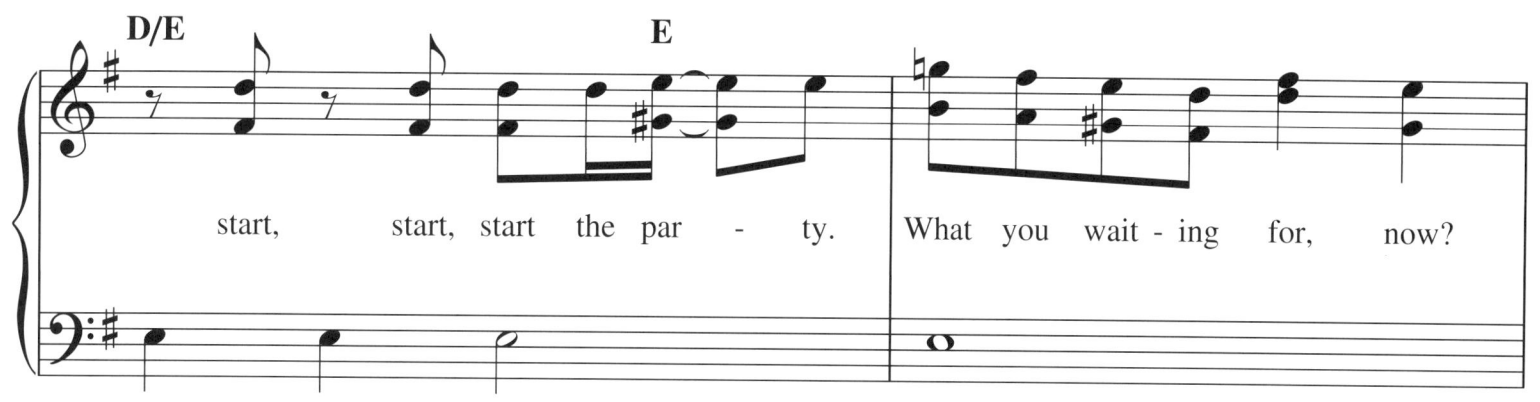
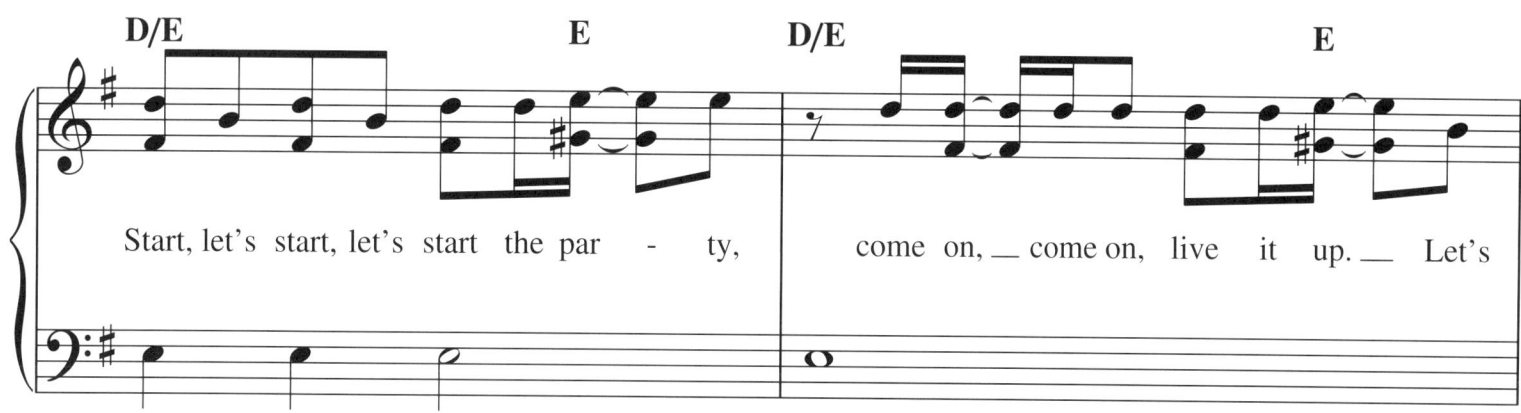
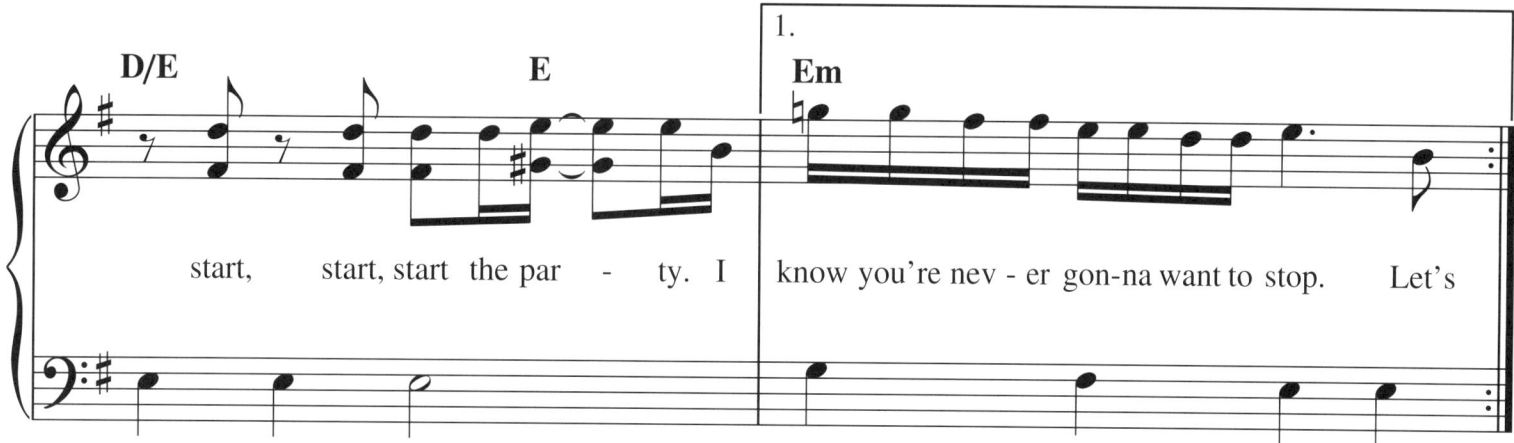

WHO WILL I BE

Words and Music by MATTHEW GERRARD
and ROBBIE NEVIL

Whoa. _____ Yeah, yeah, yeah,

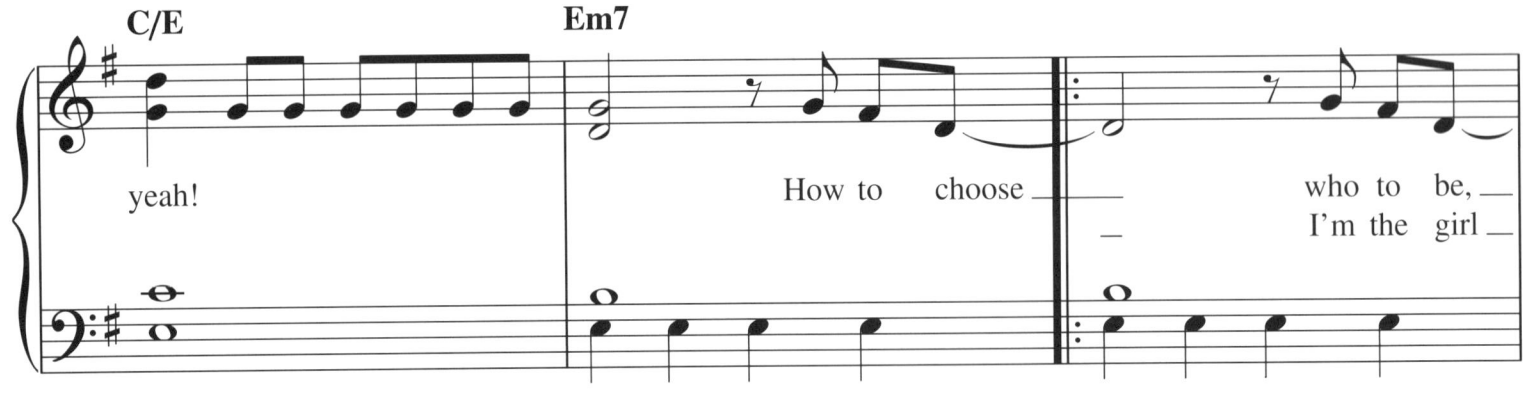

yeah! How to choose _____ who to be, _____
 I'm the girl _____

_____ well, let's see, _____ there's so man - y choic - es now. _____
to change the world, _____ I can do _____ it an - y - time. _____

© 2008 Walt Disney Music Company
All Rights Reserved   Used by Permission

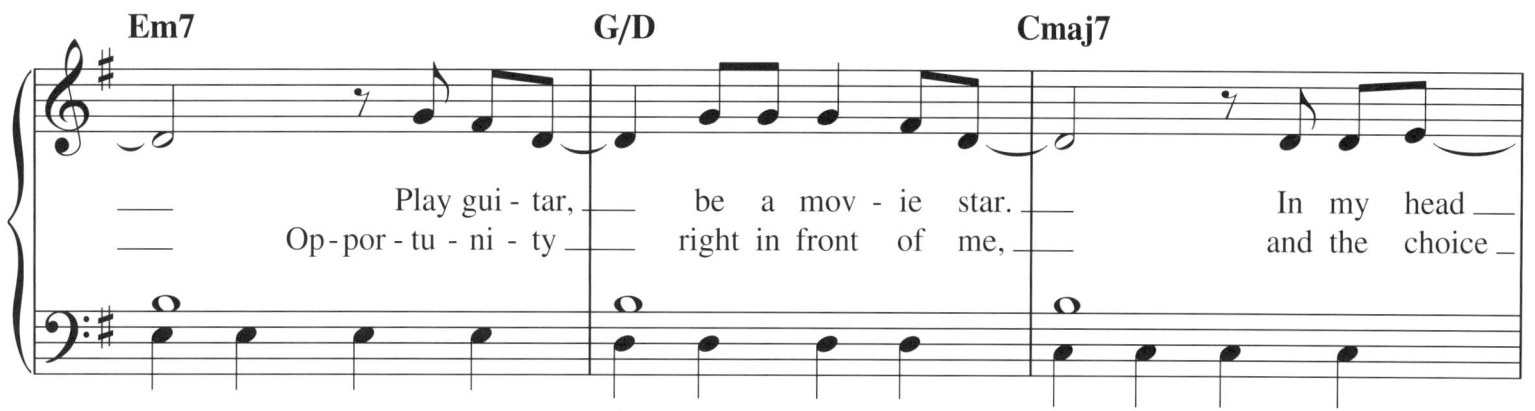
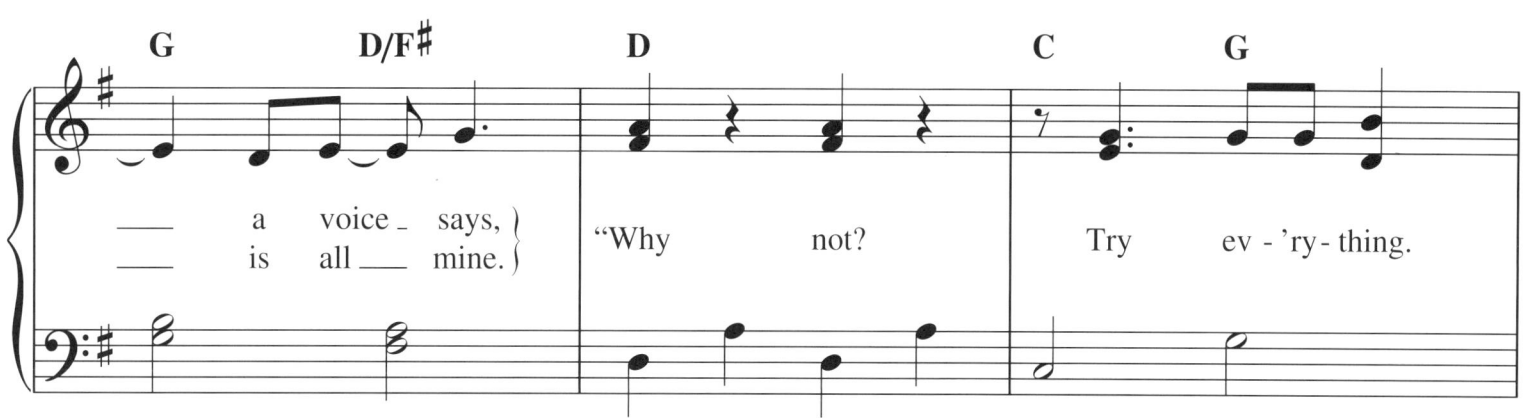

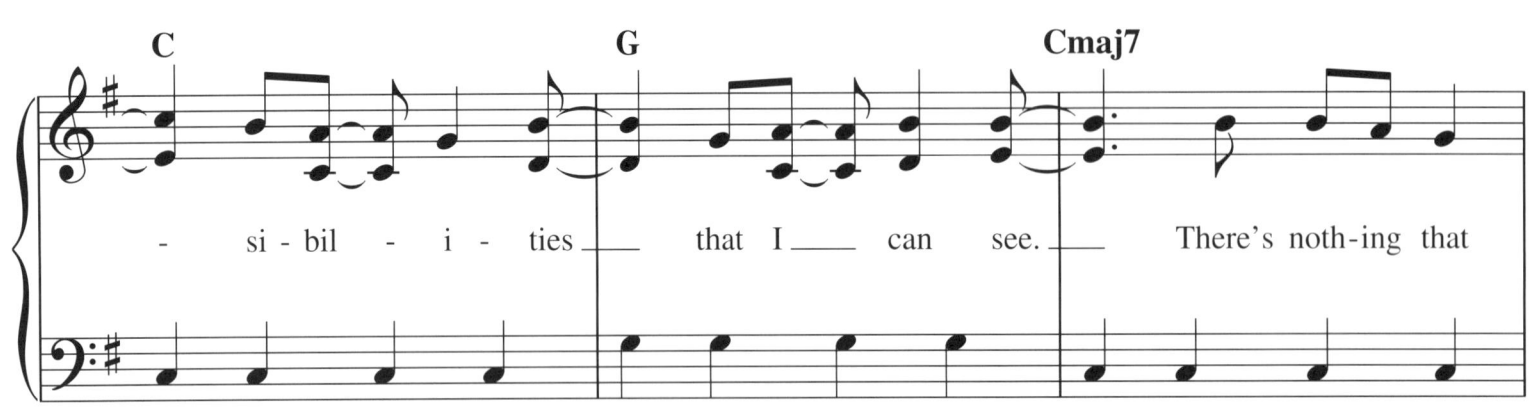

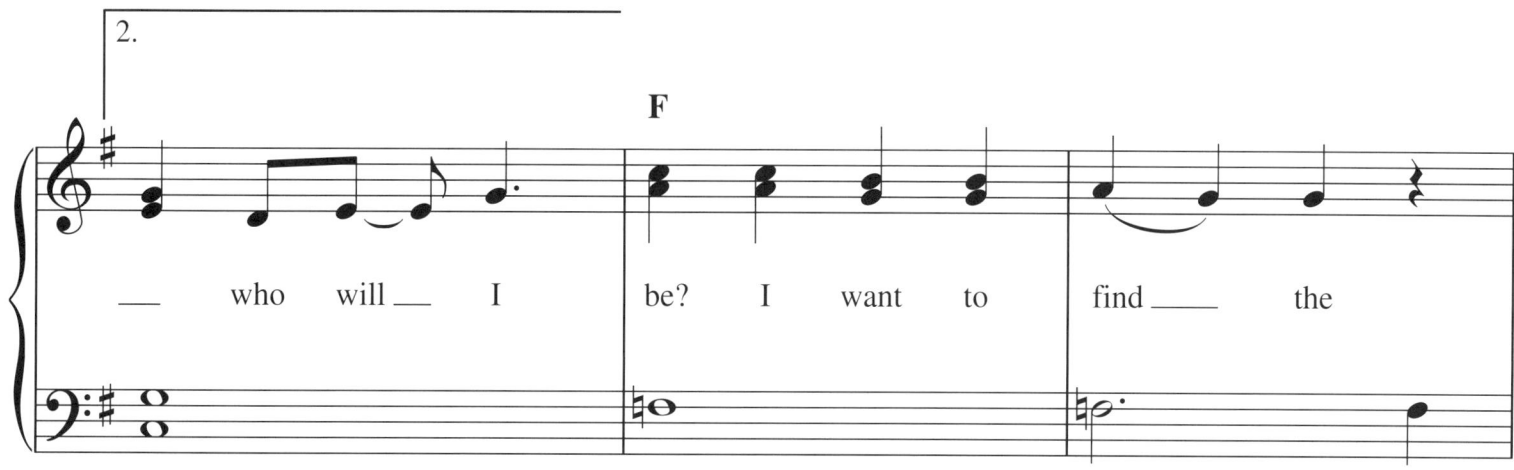

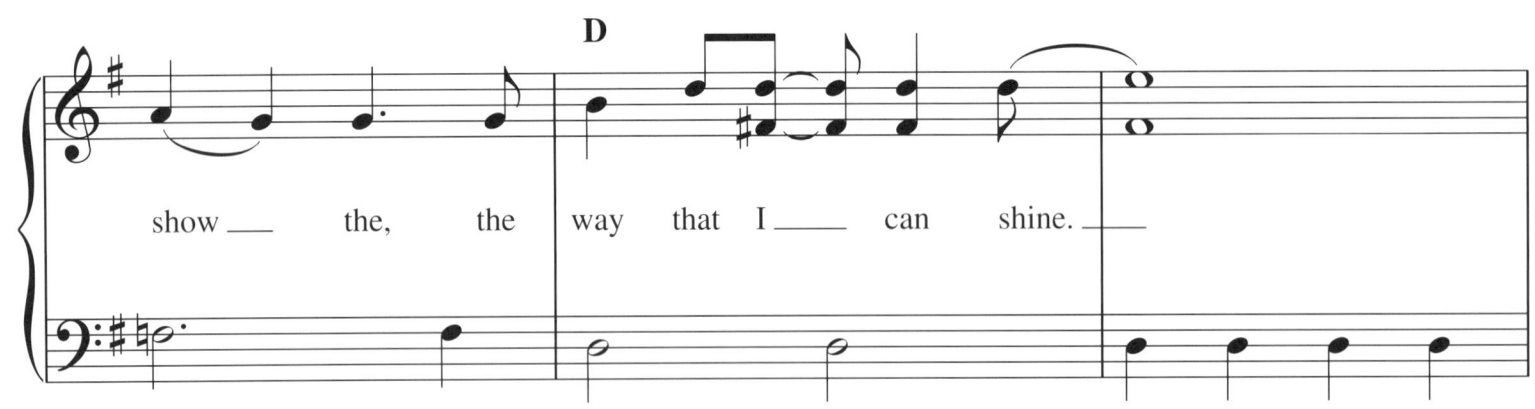

D.S. al Coda
CODA
B♭ F C D
Who will I be?
who will I be?
Em Dsus C
Whoa.
G D Em Dsus
Who will I be?
B♭ F C D G
(Spoken:) Who will I be?

THIS IS ME

Words and Music by ADAM WATTS
and ANDY DODD

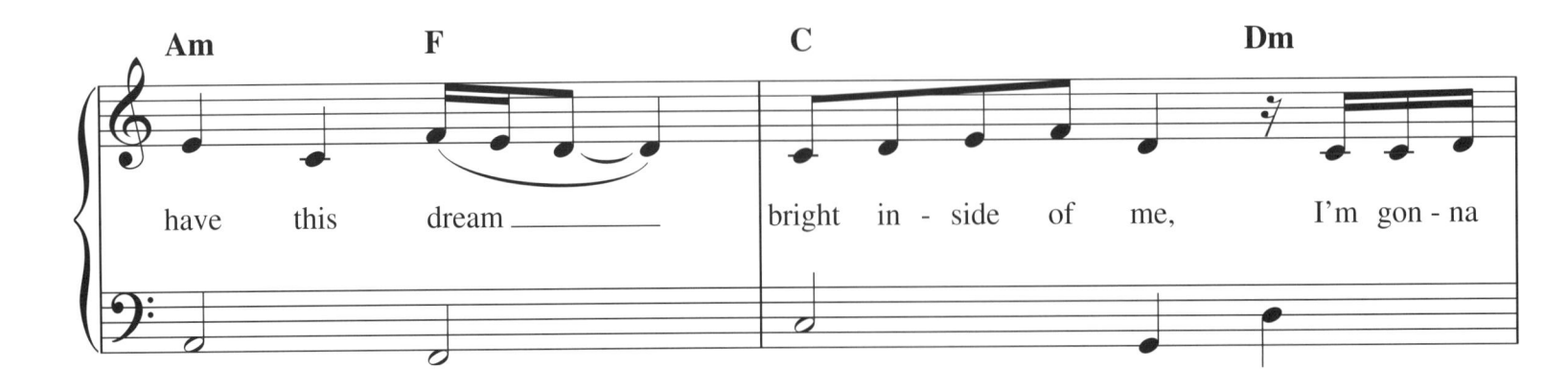

Pop Rock

I've always been the kind of girl that hid my face, so afraid to tell the world what I've got to say. But I have this dream bright inside of me, I'm gonna

© 2008 Walt Disney Music Company
All Rights Reserved   Used by Permission

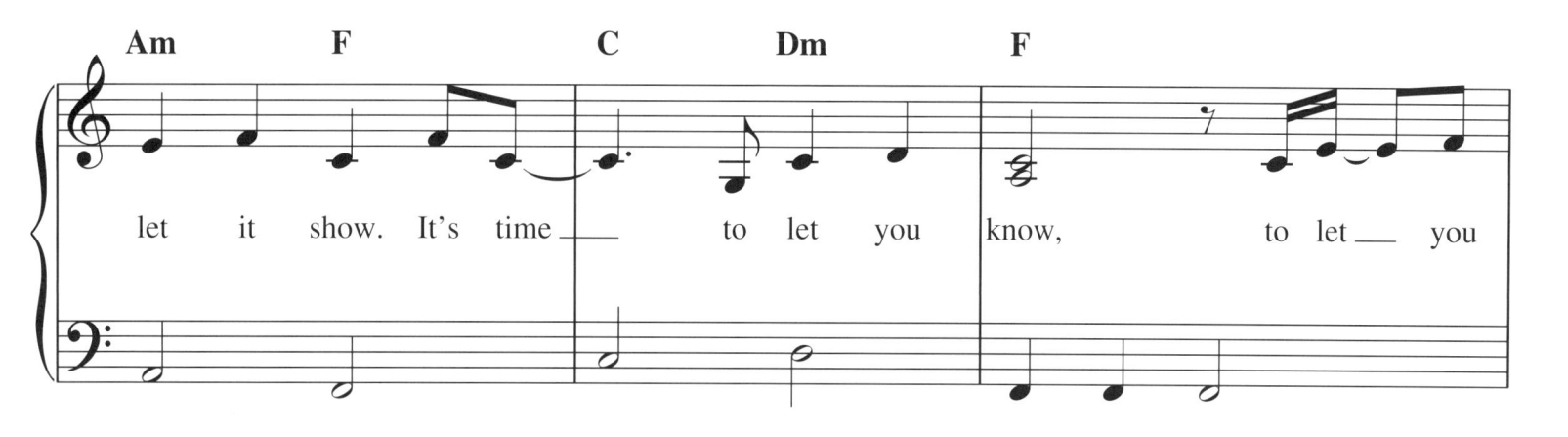

let it show. It's time to let you know, to let you know. This is real, this is me, I'm exact-ly where I'm sup-posed to be, now. Gon-na let the light shine on me. Now I've found who I am, there's no

C G Dm7 To Coda
way to hold it in.
No more hid - ing who I want to
F G Am F C G
be, this is me. Do you
Am F C Dm
know what it's like to feel so in the dark, to
Am F C Dm
dream a - bout a life where you're the shin - ing star? E - ven

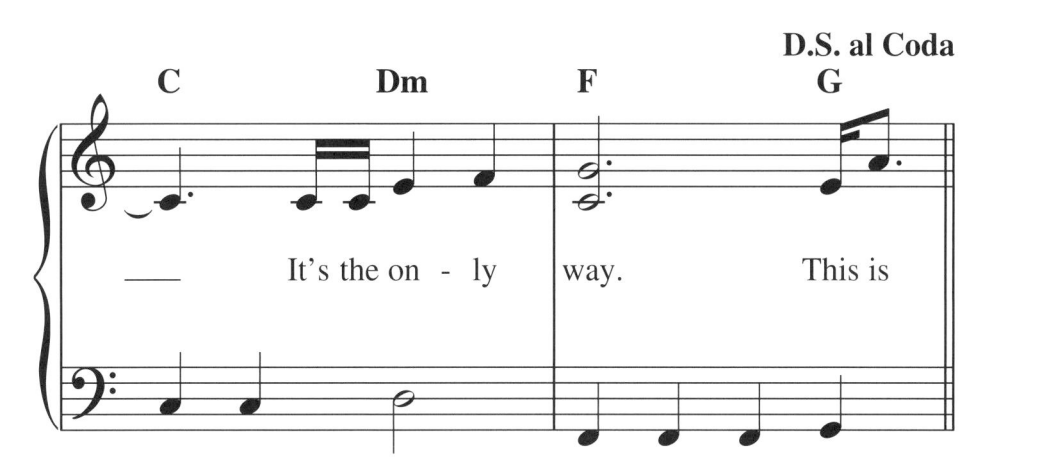

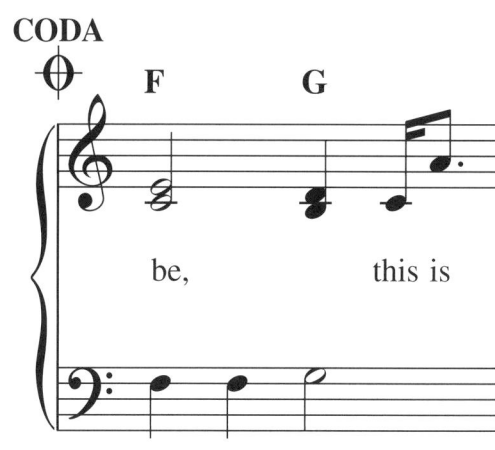

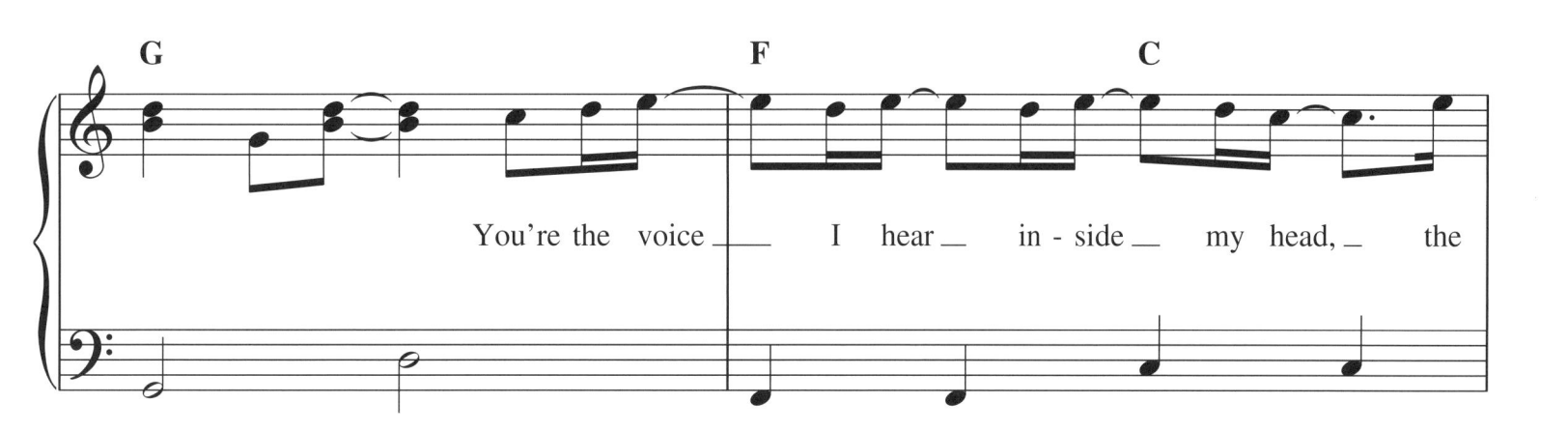

| Am | F | C | Dm | Am | F |

though it seems like it's too far a-way, I have to be-lieve in my-self.

| C | Dm | F | **D.S. al Coda** G | **CODA** F | G |

It's the on-ly way. This is be, this is

| Am | F | C | Dm | Am | F |

me.

| G | | F | C |

You're the voice I hear in-side my head, the

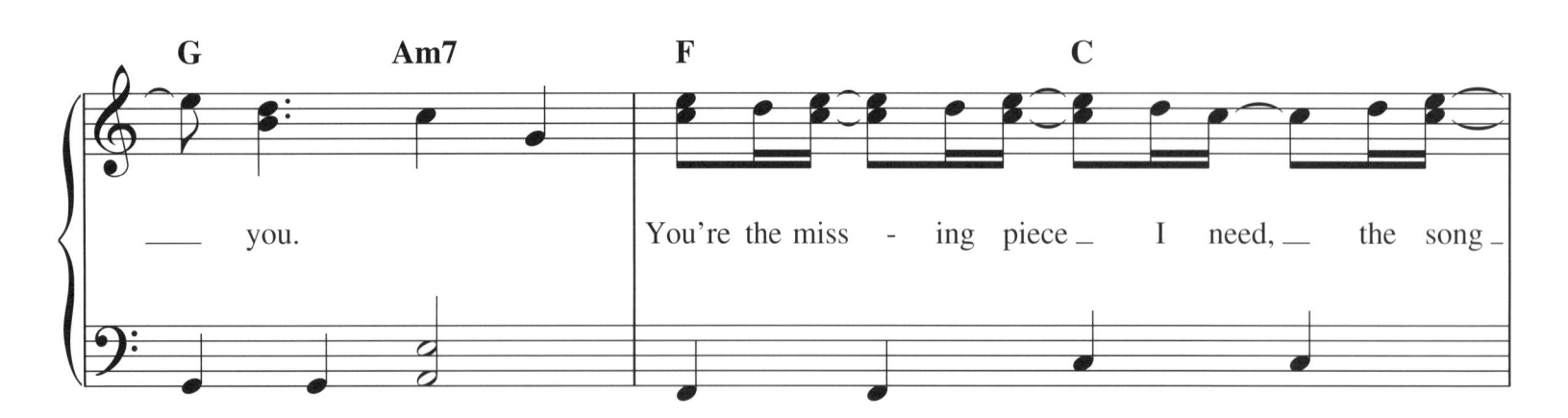

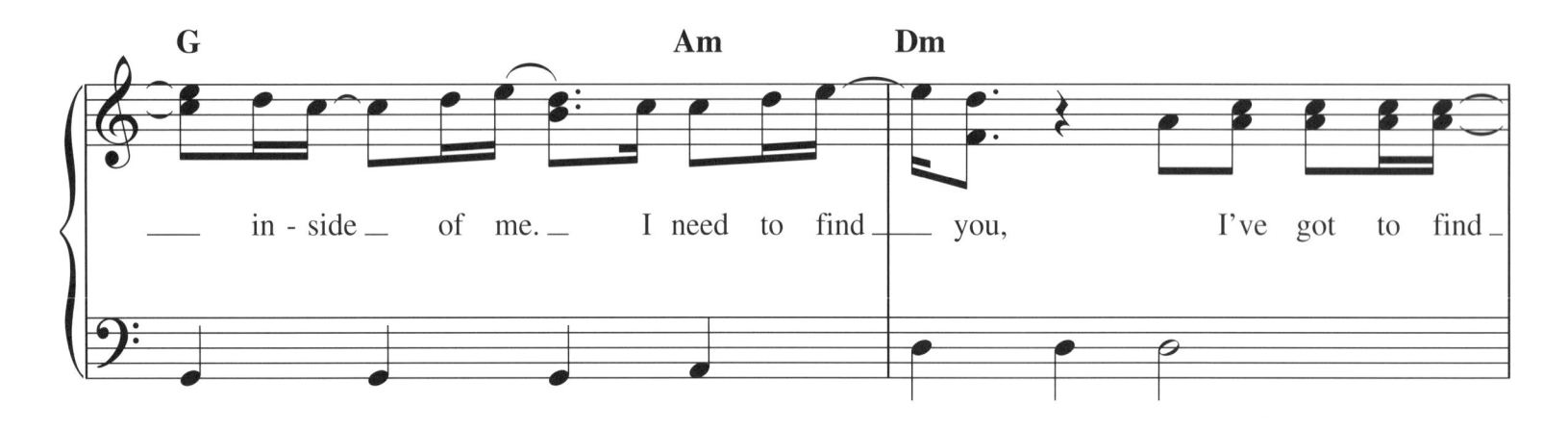

rea - son that I'm sing - ing. I need to find you, I've got to find you.

You're the miss - ing piece I need, the song inside of me. I need to find you, I've got to find you.

This is real, this is me, I'm ex-

G Am F C
act - ly where I'm sup - posed to be, now. Gon-na let the light
G Am7 F
shine on me. Now I've found who I am, there's no
C G Dm7
way to hold it in. No more hid - ing who I want to be,
F G F C
this is me.
You're the miss - ing piece I need, the song

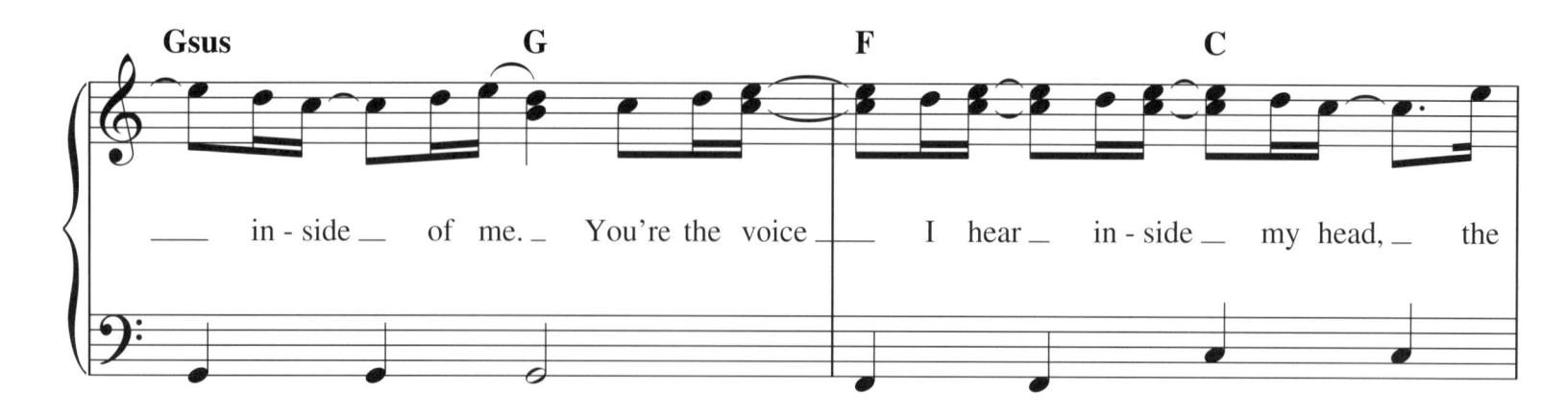

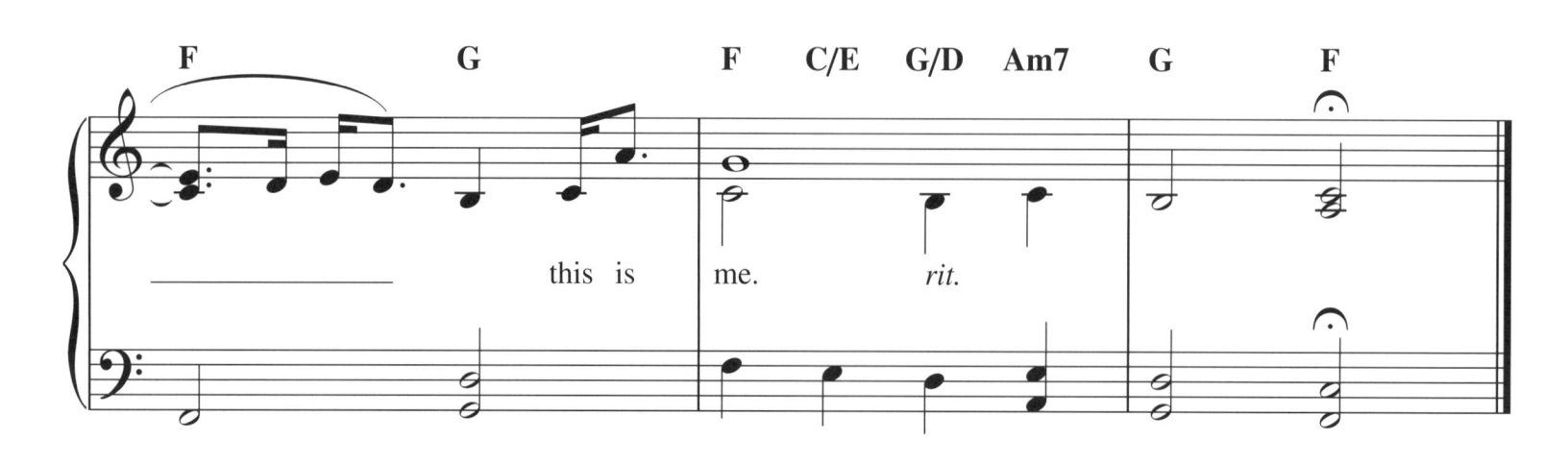

_____ in - side _____ of me. _____ You're the voice _____ I hear _____ in - side _____ my head, _____ the rea - son that _____ I'm sing - ing. Now I've found who I am, there's no way to hold _____ it in. _____ No more hid - ing who I want to be, _____ this is me. *rit.*

HASTA LA VISTA

Words and Music by TOBY GAD,
PAM SHEYNE and KOVASCIAR MYVETTE

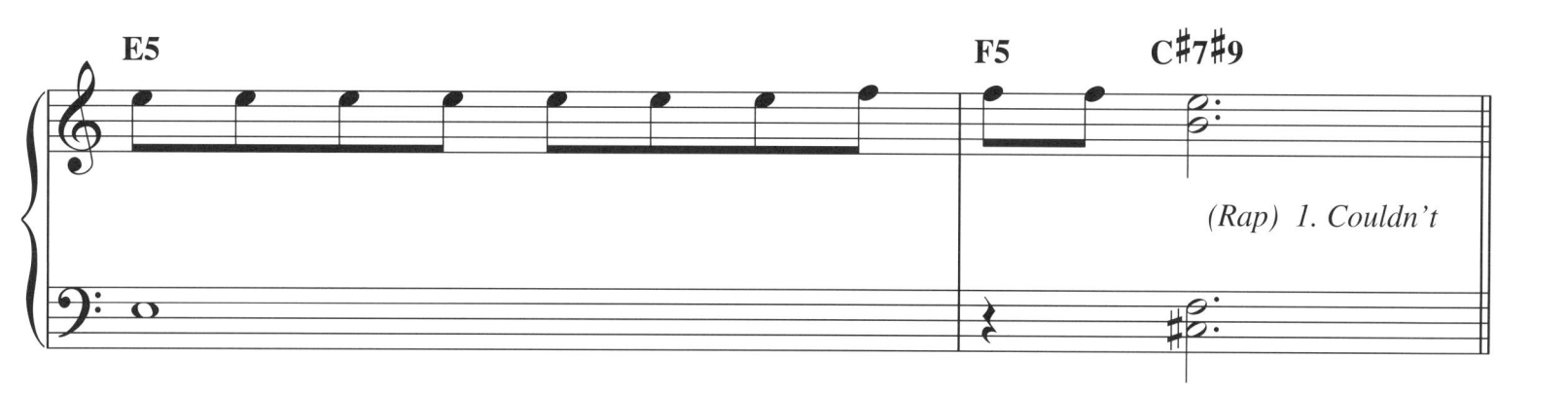

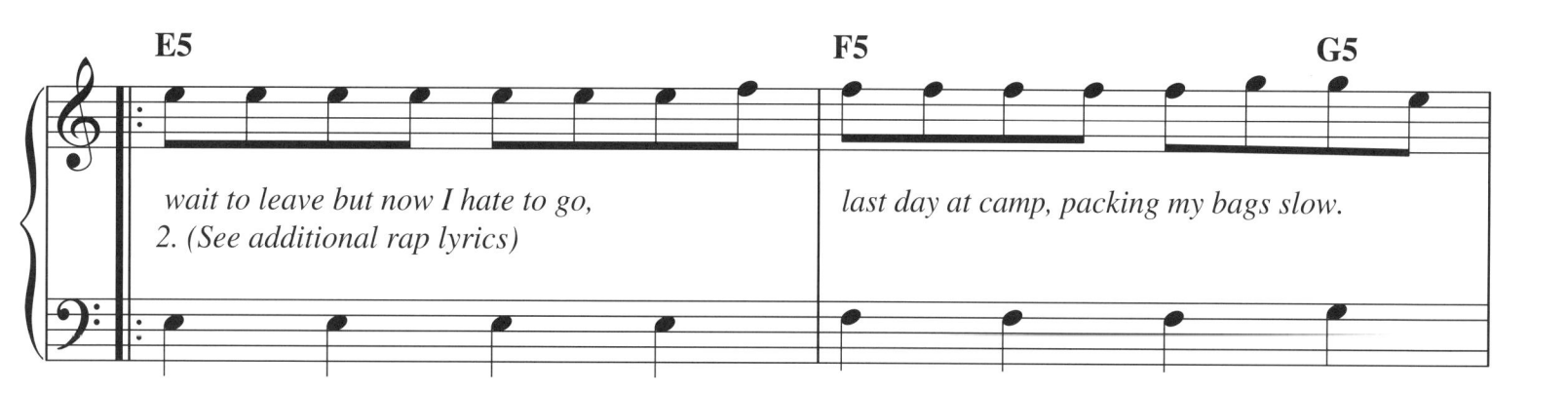

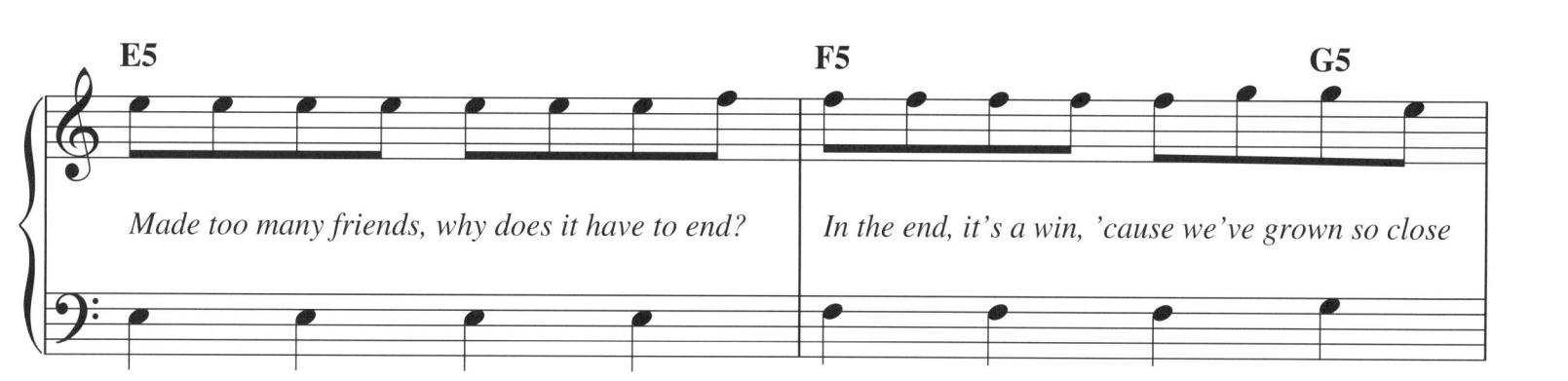

Moderate Hip-Hop feel

mf

(Rap) 1. Couldn't

wait to leave but now I hate to go,
2. (See additional rap lyrics)

last day at camp, packing my bags slow.

Made too many friends, why does it have to end?

In the end, it's a win, 'cause we've grown so close

© 2008 Walt Disney Music Company and Wonderland Music Company, Inc.
All Rights Reserved   Used by Permission

together. Remember when we first met, first day? *Figured this would be no fun, no way. And now*

it's time to leave, but now we want to stay, stay, *stay, stay, stay, stay, oh.*

𝄋 Chorus

Has - ta la vis - ta, I'm gon-na say good - bye to you, what-ev-er hap-pens, I'll be

cool with you. Wan-na give me your num - ber, I'm a call you, prom-ise I won't for-get you.

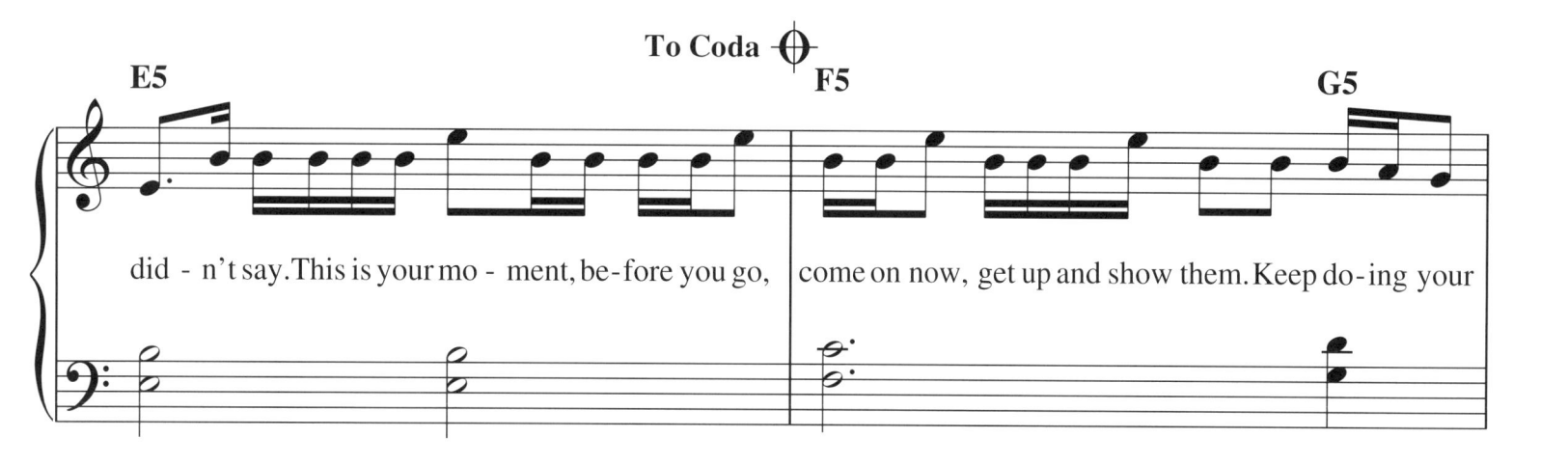

Has-ta la vis-ta, we'll all be go-ing sep-'rate ways, say ev-'ry-thing you did-n't say. This is your mo-ment, be-fore you go, come on now, get up and show them. Keep do-ing your thing, thing, thing, keep do-ing your thing, thing, thing. *There's so* thing, thing, thing. Keep do-ing your thing, thing, thing, keep do-ing your thing, thing, thing.

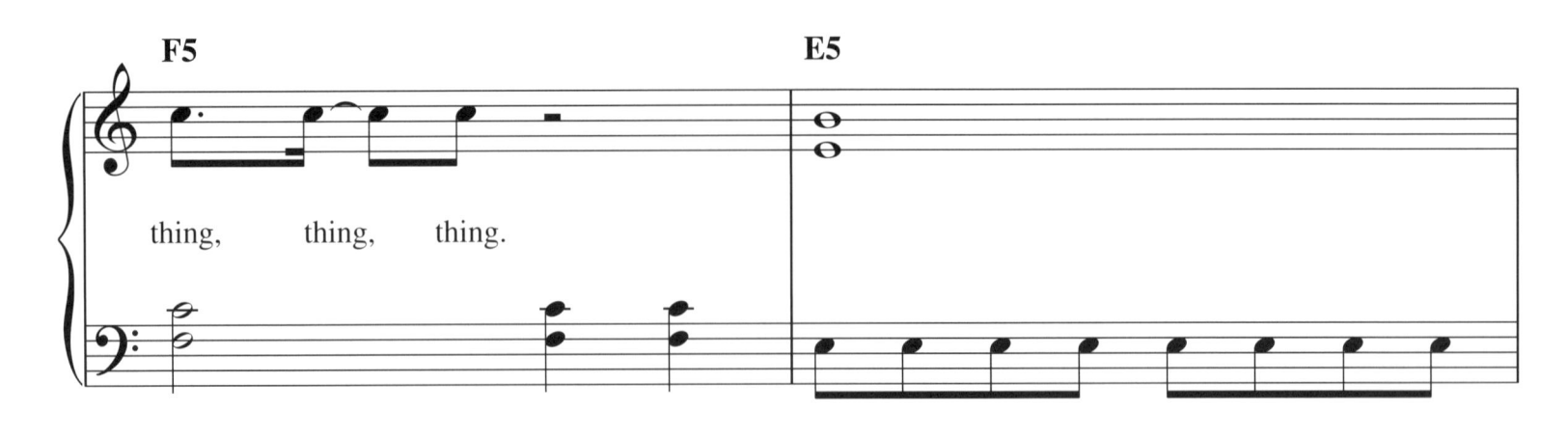

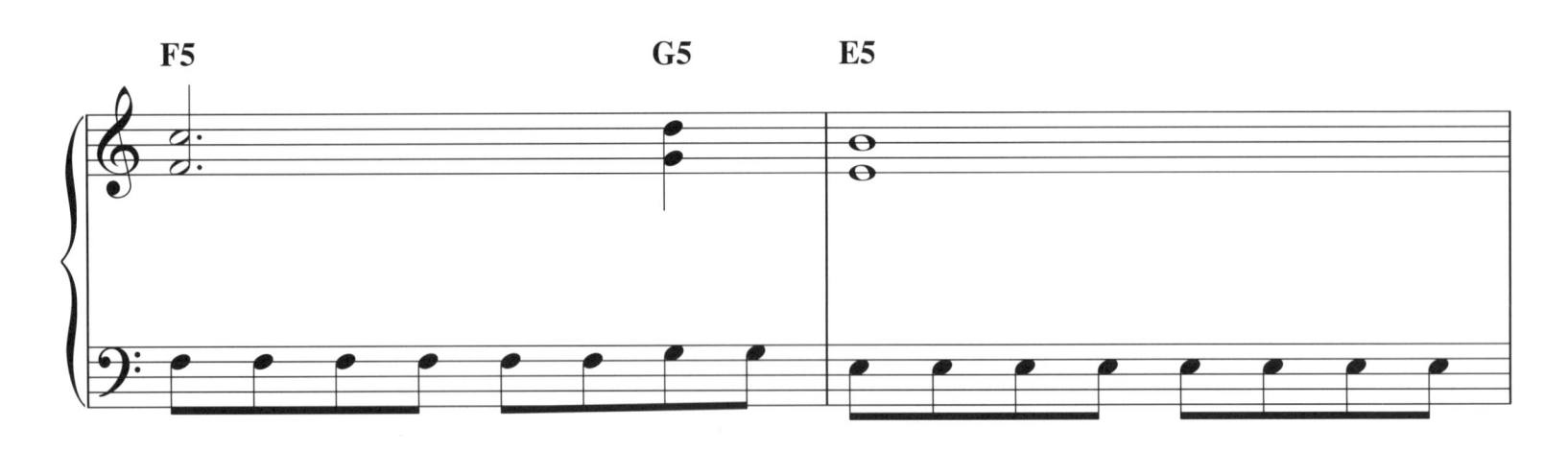

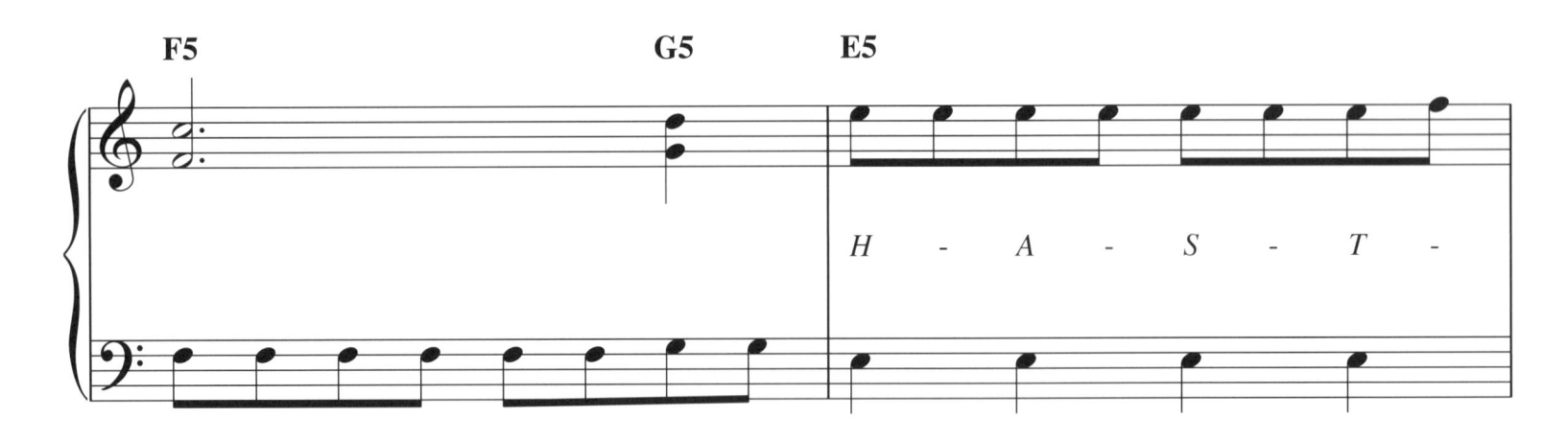

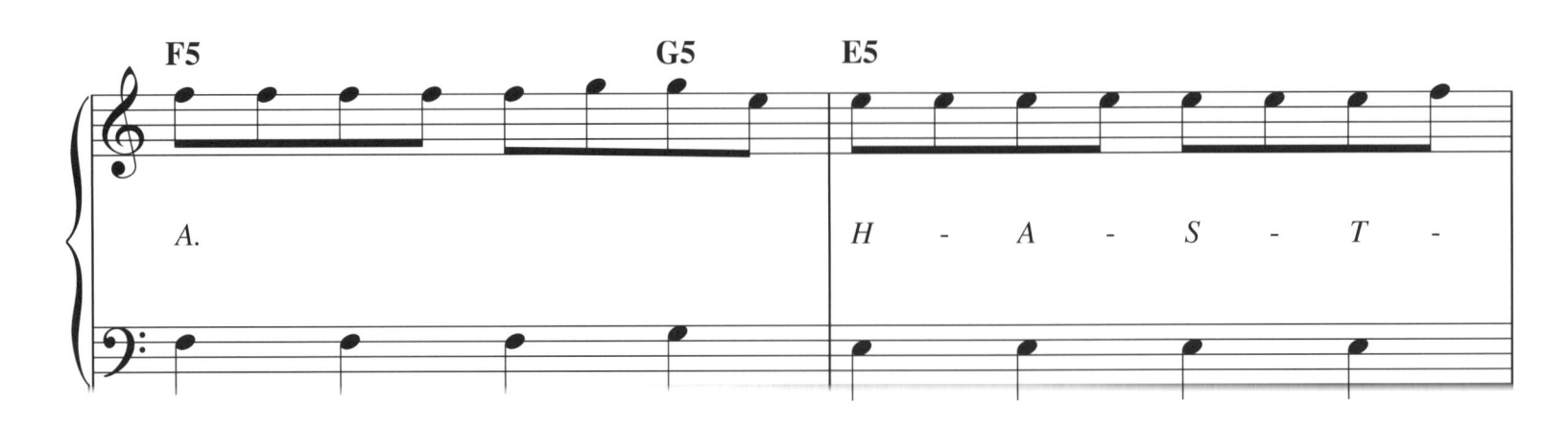

H - A - S - T -

A.

H - A - S - T -

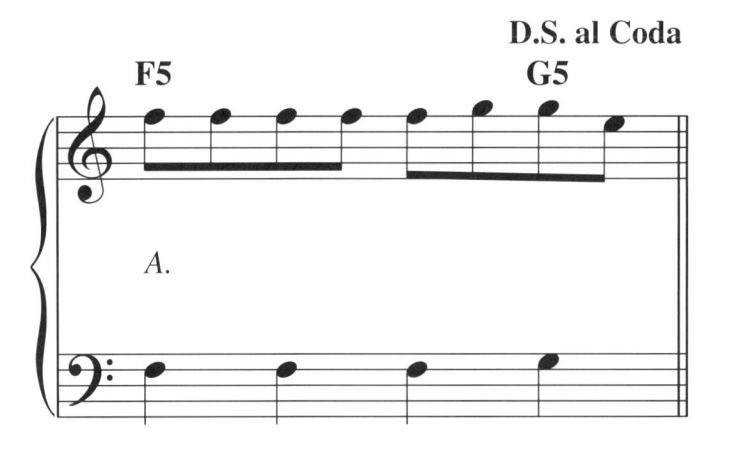

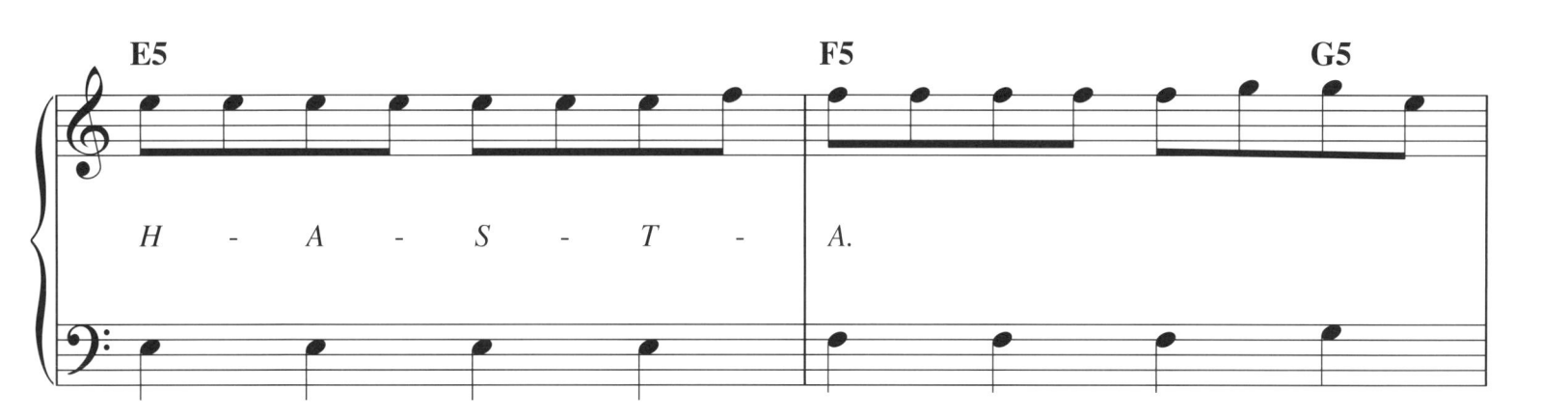

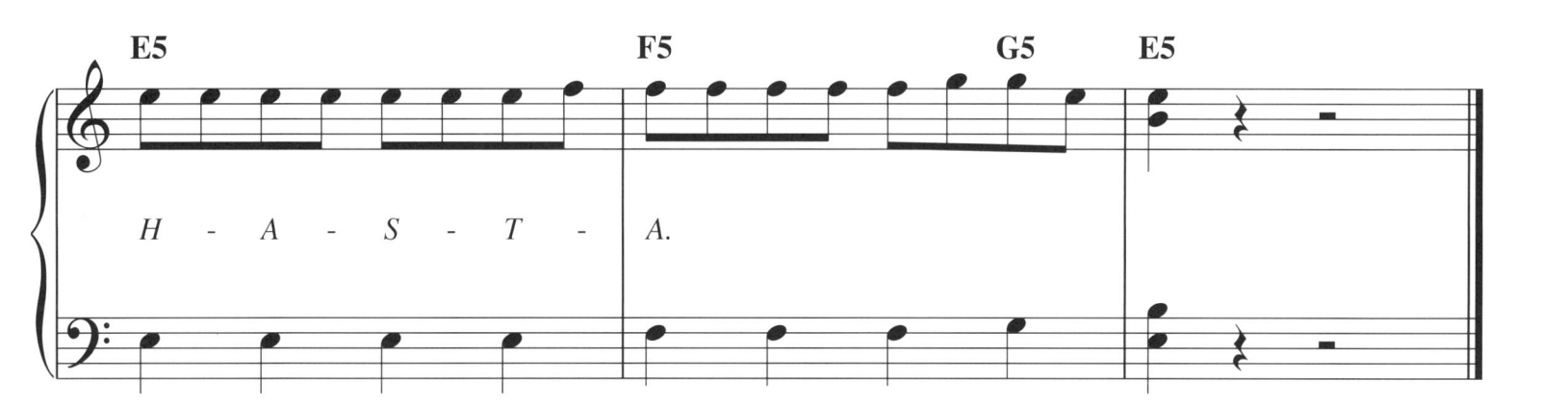

Rap Lyrics

Rap 2: There's so much more inside of me,
There's so much more I just wanna be.
All the things I've seen, obviously I'm inspired,
Got love for all the friendships I've acquired.
Everybody put a hand up,
Hey, hey, hey, hey.
Everybody put a hand up,
Hey, hey, hey, hey.
Chorus

HERE I AM

Words and Music by
JAMIE HOUSTON

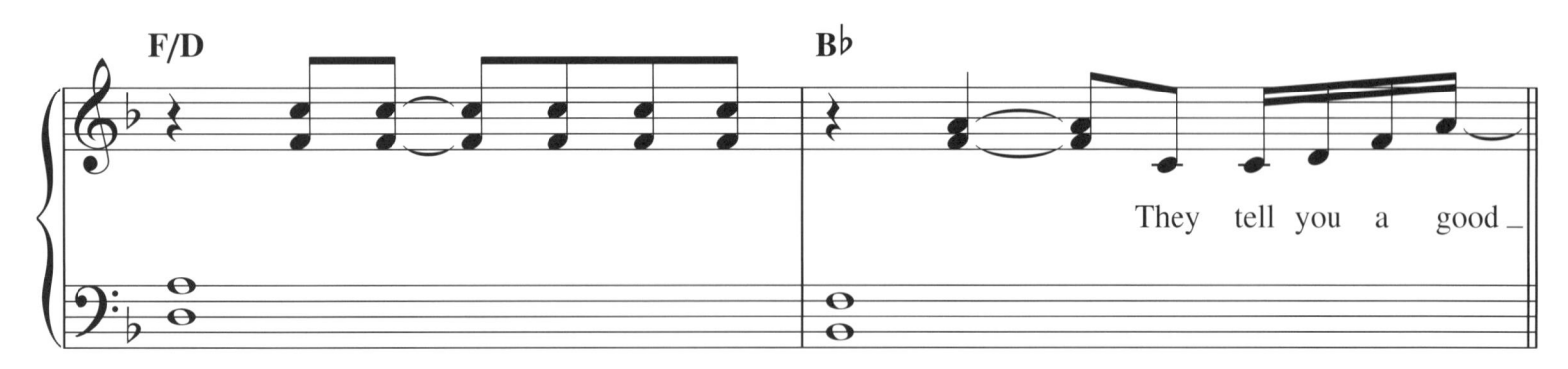

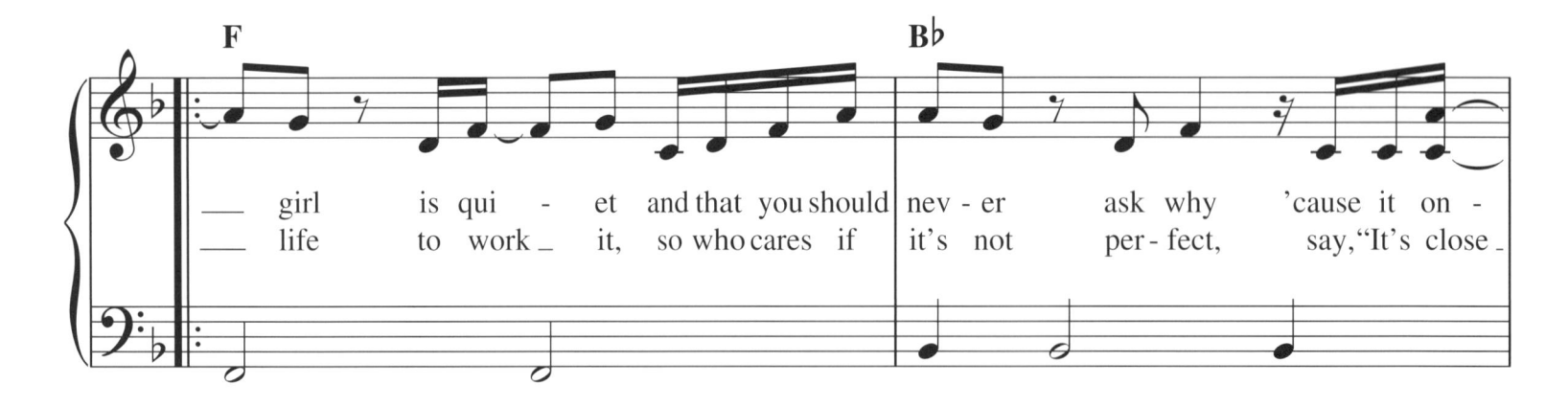

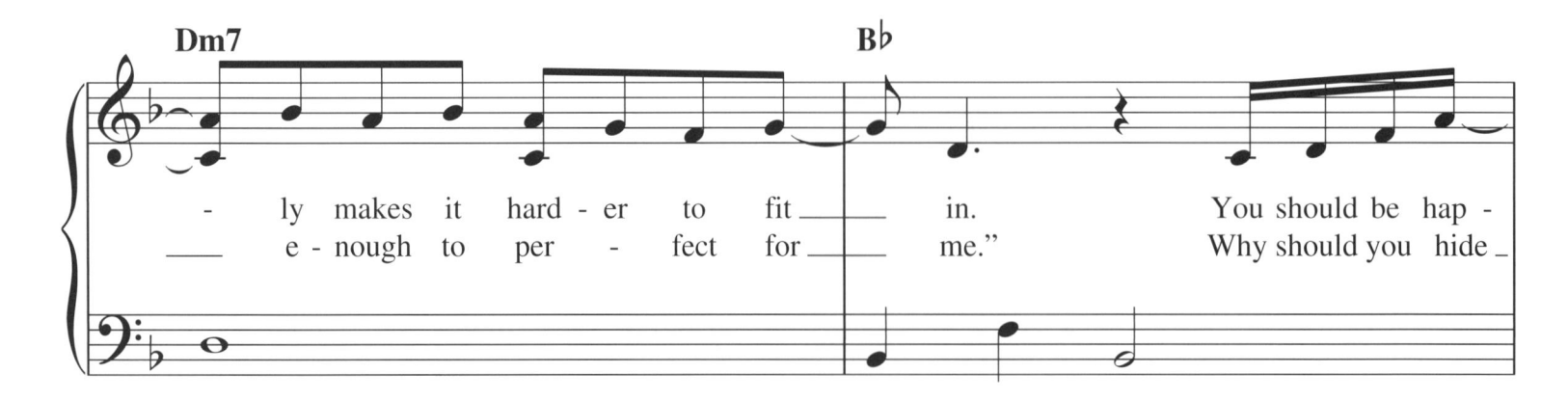

Moderate Ballad

They tell you a good _ girl is qui - et and that you should nev - er ask why 'cause it on - ly makes it hard - er to fit _ in. You should be hap -
_ life to work _ it, so who cares if it's not per - fect, say, "It's close _ e - nough to per - fect for _ me." Why should you hide _

© 2008 Walt Disney Music Company
All Rights Reserved   Used by Permission

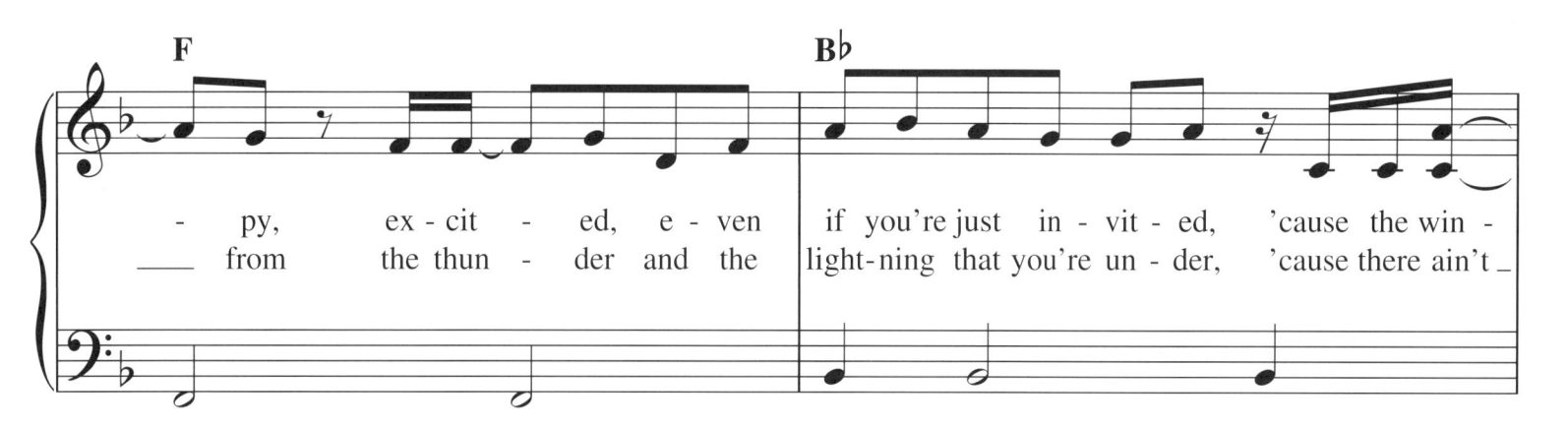

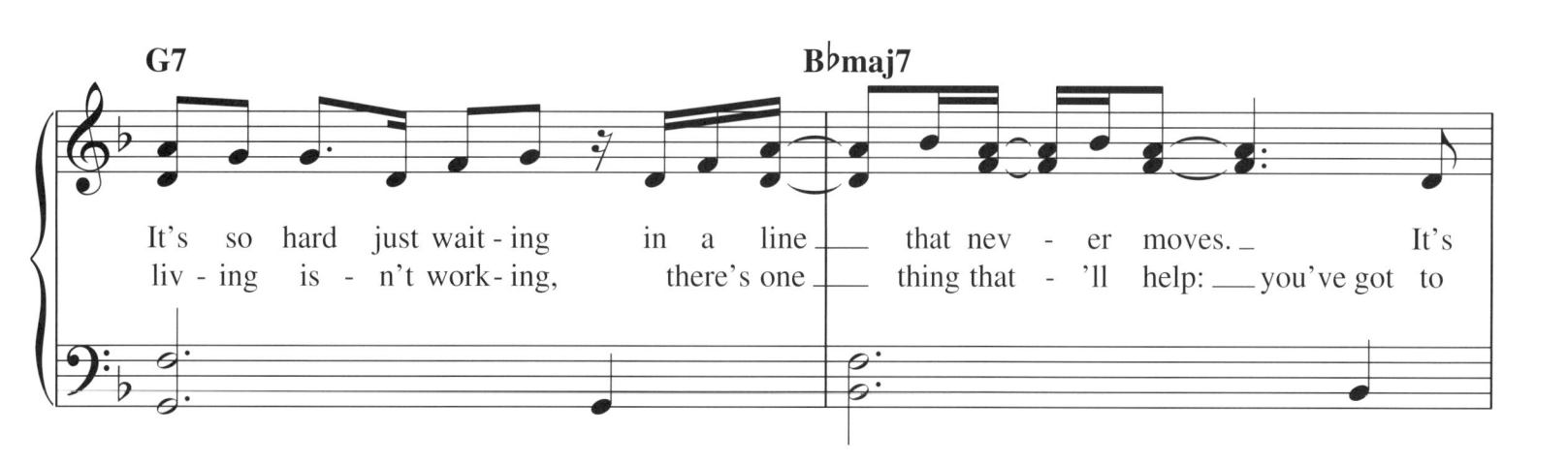

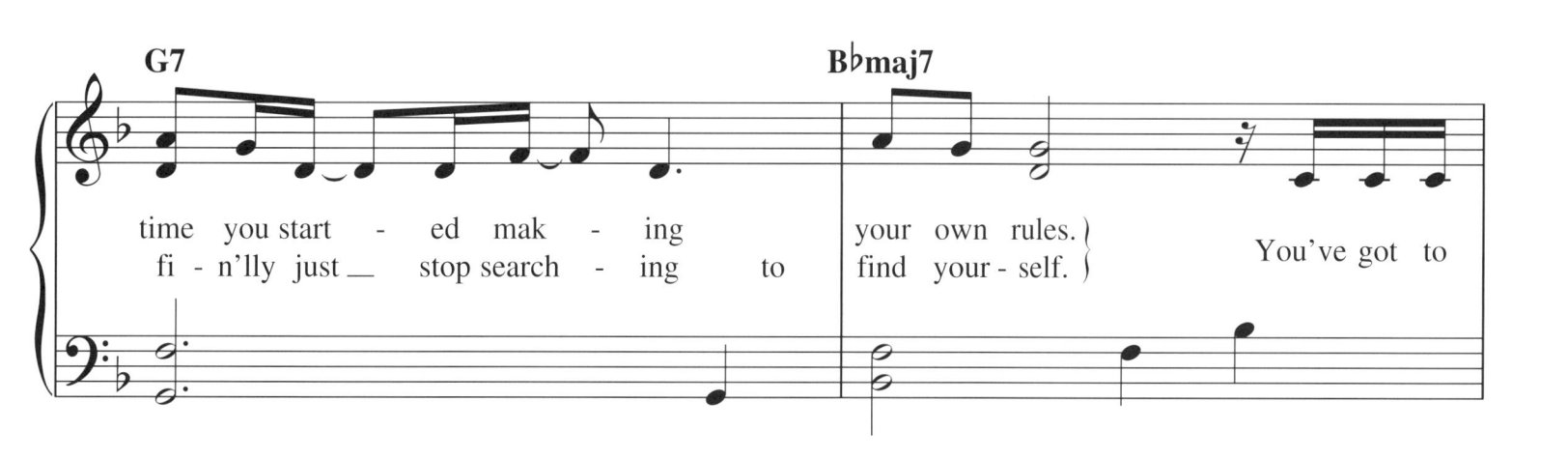

-py, ex - cit - ed, e - ven if you're just in - vit - ed, 'cause the win -
___ from the thun - der and the light-ning that you're un - der, 'cause there ain't

- ners need some - one to clap ___ for them. ___
___ no - bod - y else you want ___ to be. ___ If how you're

It's so hard just wait - ing in a line ___ that nev - er moves. ___ It's
liv - ing is - n't work - ing, there's one ___ thing that - 'll help: ___ you've got to

time you start - ed mak - ing your own rules.
fi - n'lly just ___ stop search - ing to find your - self.
You've got to

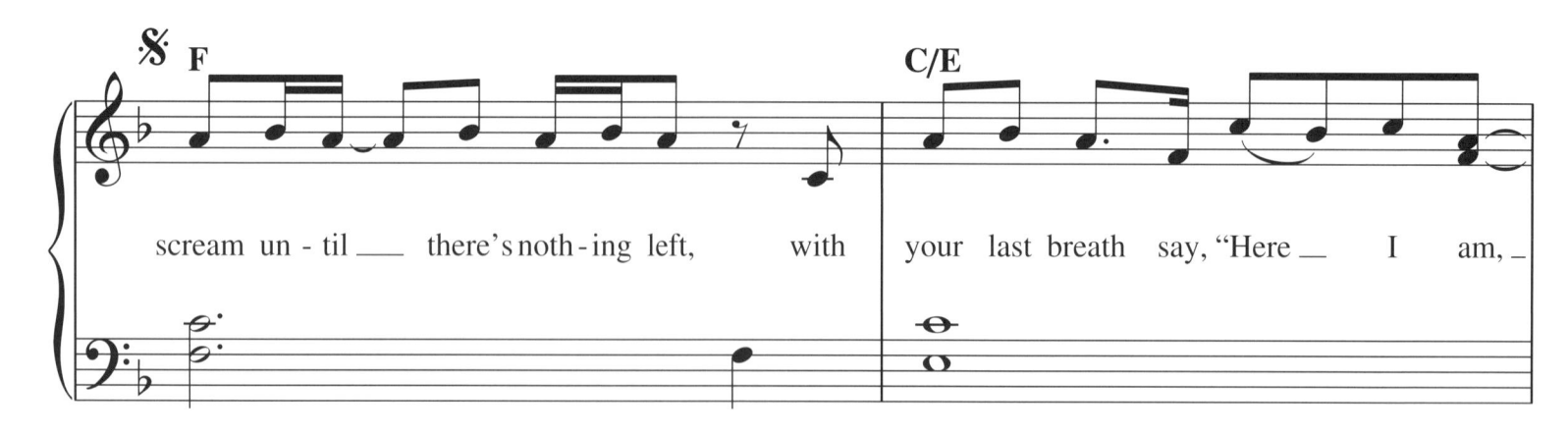

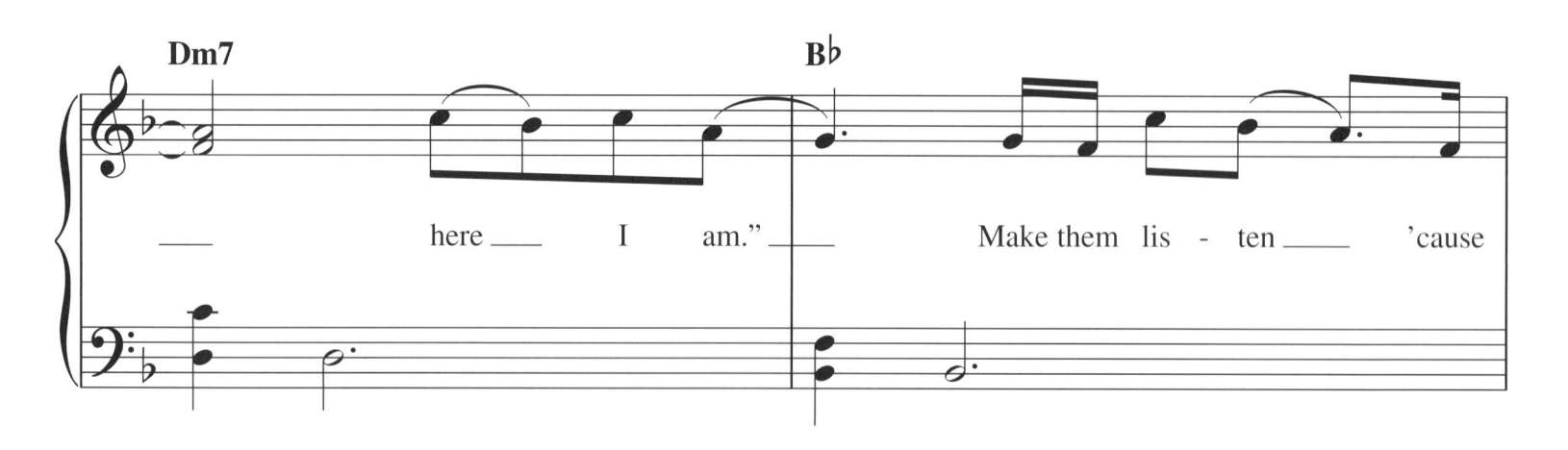

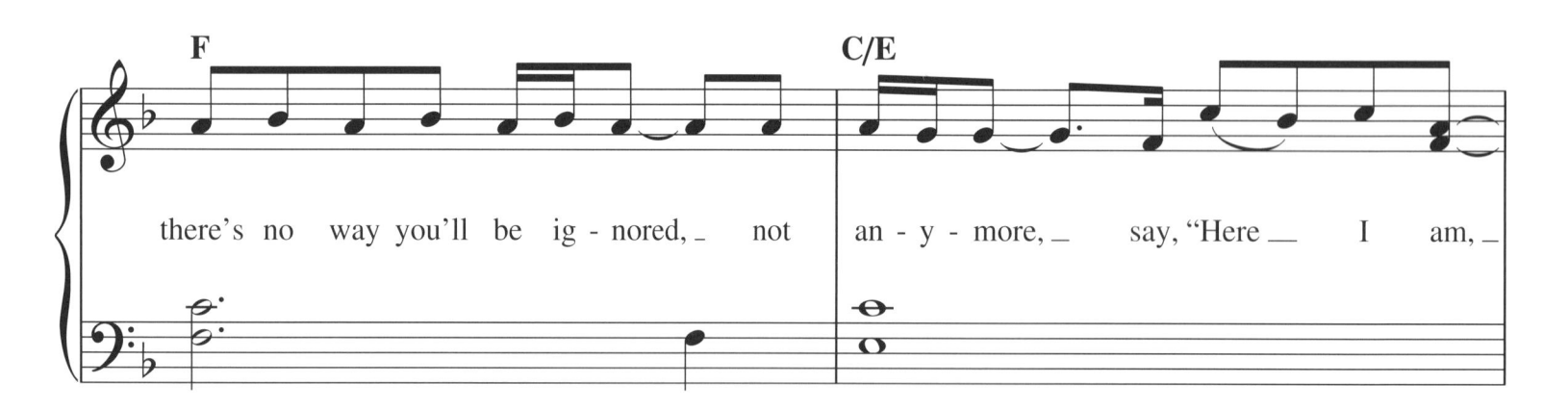

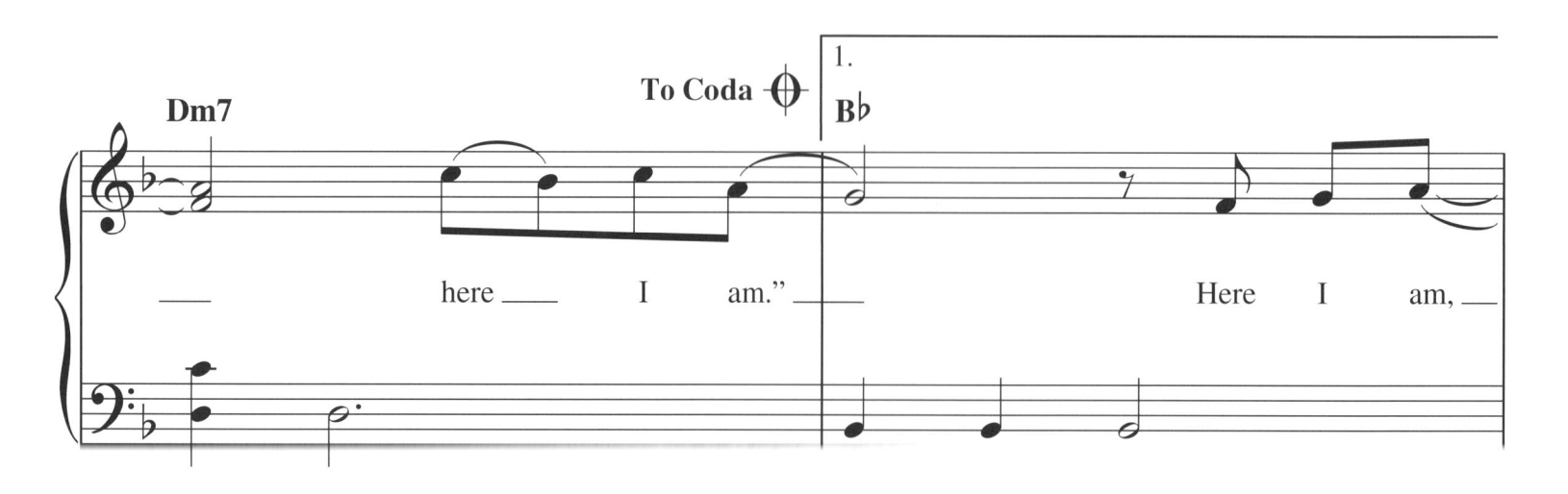

scream un-til ___ there's noth-ing left, with your last breath say, "Here __ I am, __ here __ I am." ___ Make them lis-ten ___ 'cause there's no way you'll be ig-nored, _ not an-y-more, _ say, "Here __ I am, _ here __ I am." ___ Here I am, _

F
C/E
ah, ah, ah.
Here I am,
Dm7
B♭
ah, ah.
You on - ly get one
2.
B♭
G
Here I am.
The world
B♭
G
bet - ter make some room, yeah, move o - ver, o - ver,

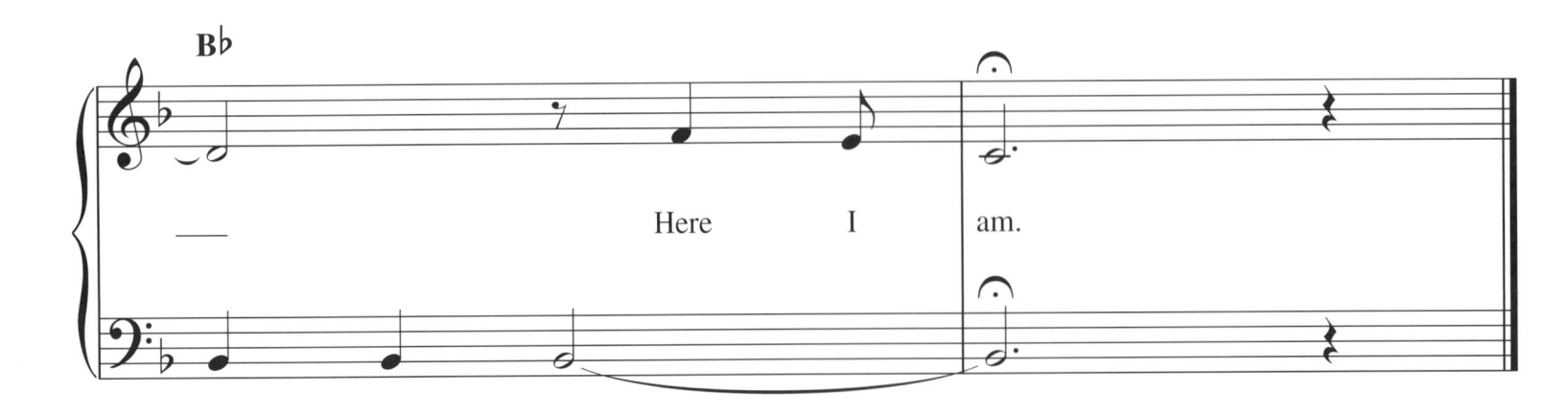

B♭

'cause you're com - ing through, __ 'cause you're com - ing through. __ Got to

D.S. al Coda

CODA

B♭   **F**

Here I am, _____ ah, ah, ah. __

C/E   **Dm7**

Here I am, _____ ah, ah, ah. __

B♭

Here I am.

TOO COOL

Words and Music by TOBY GAD
and PAM SHEYNE

Dance Pop

mf

I'm too cool for my dress, these shades don't leave my
nice, e - ven I'm sur -

head. Ev - 'ry - thing you say is so ir - rel -
prised, you are still al - lowed to be in my

e - vant. You fol - low and I lead, you want to be like
crew. I'll show you how it's done if you want to be some -

© 2008 Walt Disney Music Company and Wonderland Music Company, Inc.
All Rights Reserved   Used by Permission

B♭5 F G5 E♭5
me, but you're just a wan - na - be, love it or hate
one; just watch me and you'll learn
B♭ F G5 E♭ B♭ F
it. I can't help the way I am,
some. Me, my - self and I a - gree,
G5 E♭ B♭
hope you don't mis - un - der - stand. But I'm too
you'll nev - er catch up with me. 'Cause
Gm E♭ B♭/D F Gm E♭
cool, too cool, and I'm too cool to know

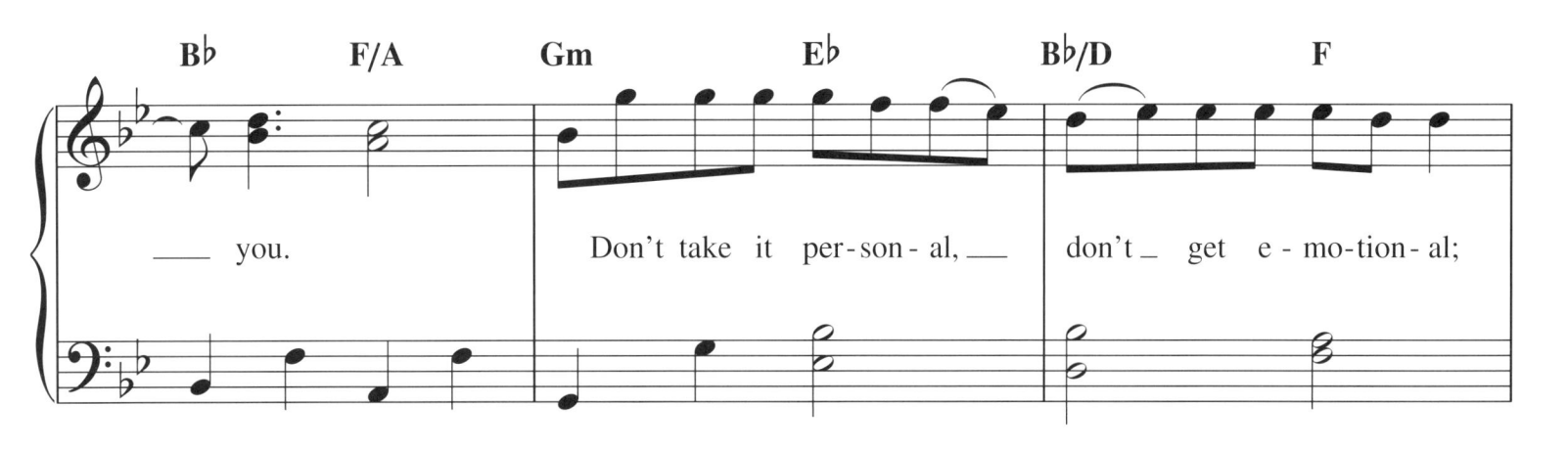

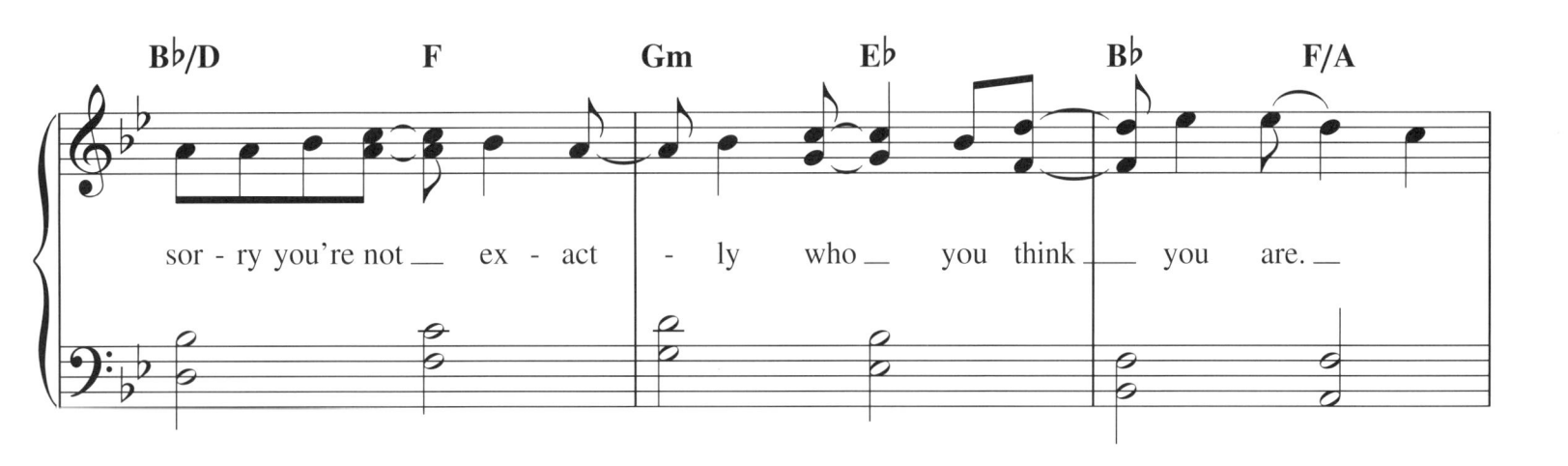

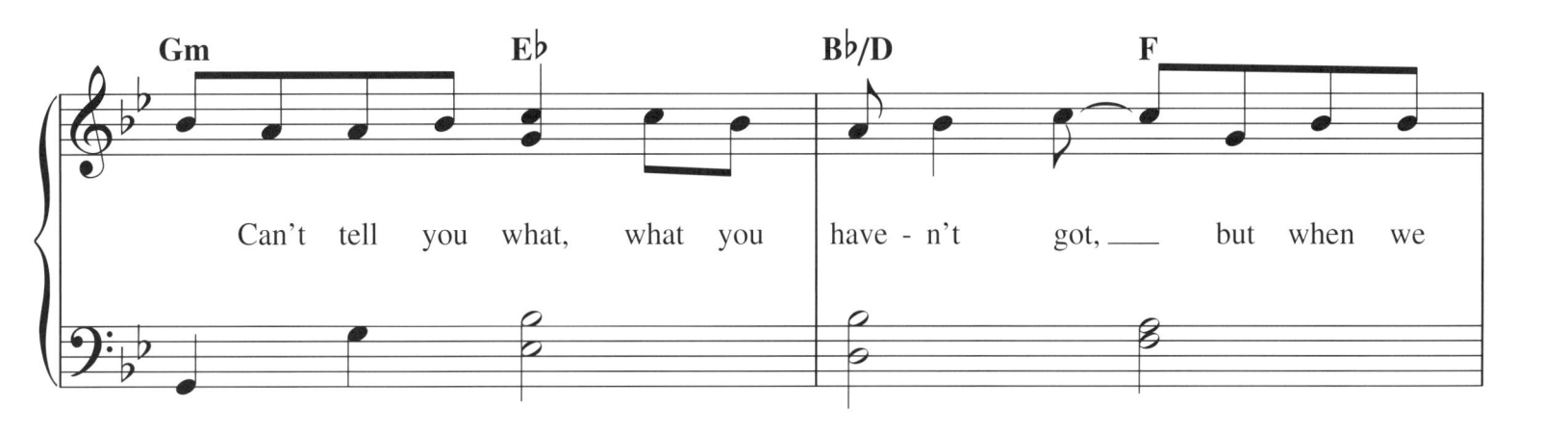

___ you. Don't take it per-son-al, ___ don't ___ get e-mo-tion-al; you know it's ___ the truth, I'm too cool ___ for you. ___ You think you're hot, but I'm sor-ry you're not ___ ex-act-ly who ___ you think ___ you are. ___ Can't tell you what, what you have-n't got, ___ but when we

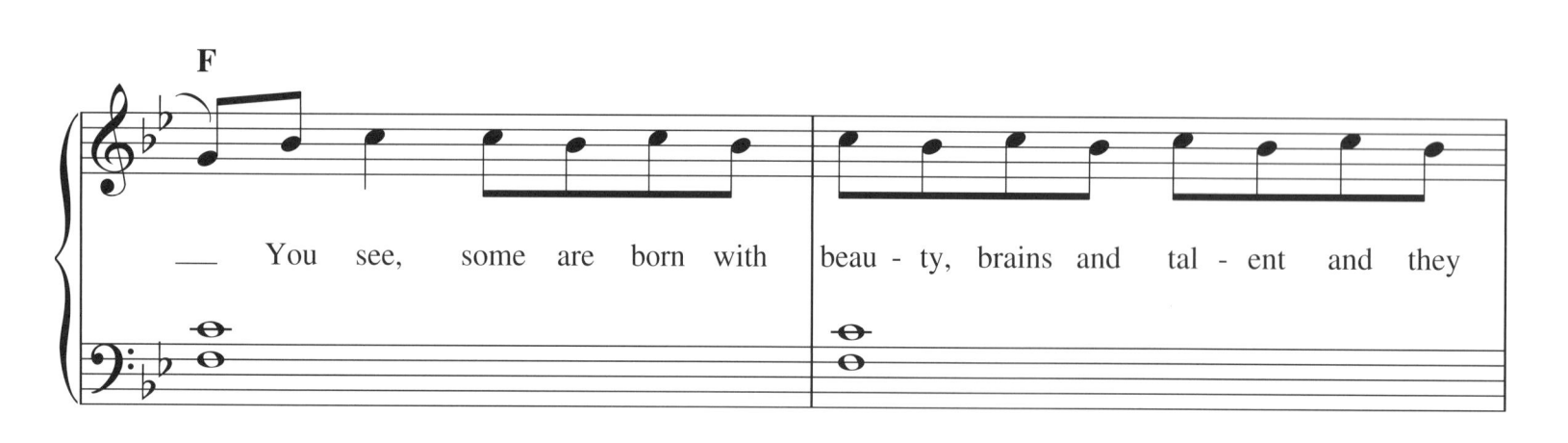

walk in-to the room, I'm too cool for you. I'm too cool for you. You're luck-y I'm so I'm too cool for you. You see, some are born with beau-ty, brains and tal-ent and they got it all. While oth-ers have to try all__ their lives,_ still they nev - er get__ the call.

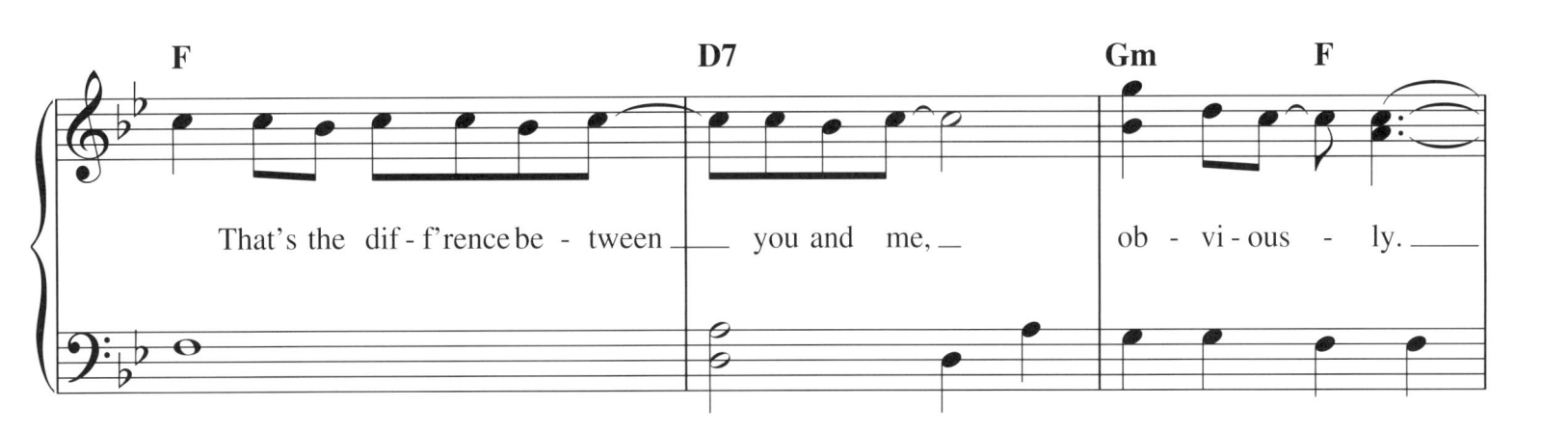

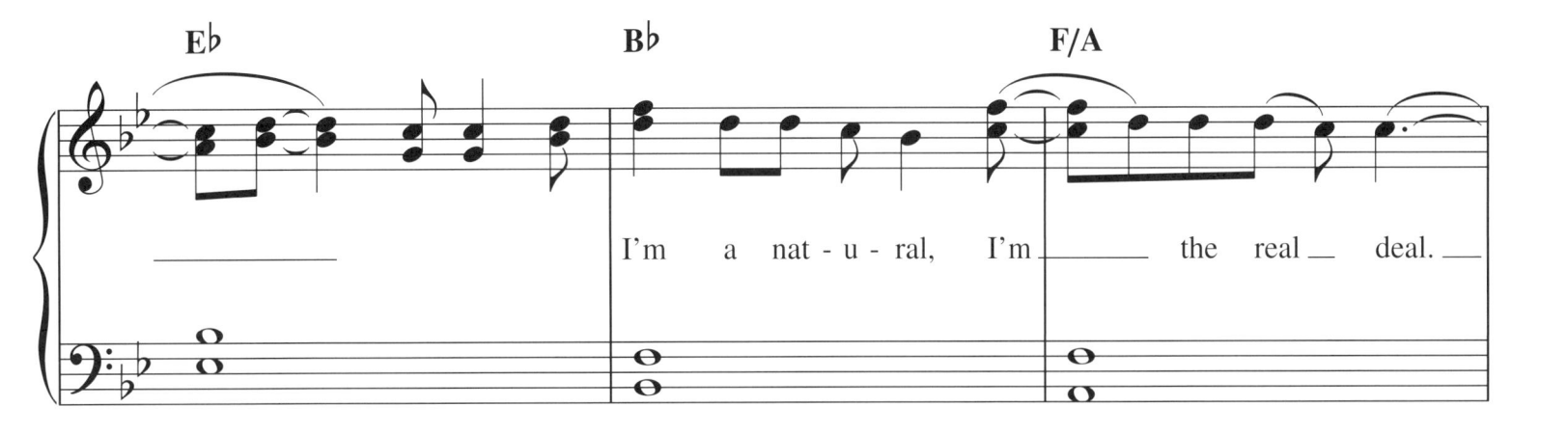

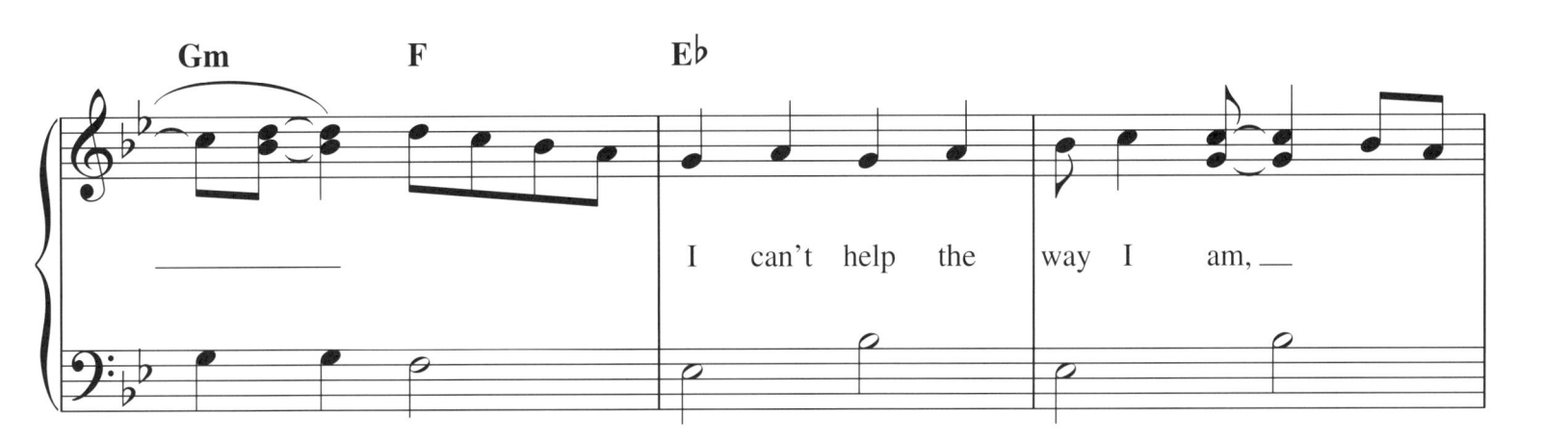

That's the dif - f'rence be - tween__ you and me,_ ob - vi - ous - ly._

I'm a nat - u - ral, I'm__ the real_ deal._

I can't help the way I am,_

Gm/F
hope you don't mis - un - der - stand. But I'm too
Gm Eb
cool, too
Bb/D F
cool, and I'm too
Gm Eb
cool to know
Bb F/A
you.
Gm Eb
Don't take it per - son - al,
Bb/D F
don't get e - mo - tion - al;
Cm7 Bb/D
you know it's the truth,
1.
Eb F
I'm too cool. Too
2.
Eb F
I'm too cool for
Gm
you.

OUR TIME IS HERE

Words and Music by TIM JAMES
and ANTONINA ARMATO

B♭maj7
F
It keeps get - ting strong - er; don't
The road keeps on turn - ing and
Dm
C6
be a - fraid, we'll do it to - geth - er.
all we can do is trav - el each day to the next.
B♭
F
Dm
Come on, come on, you know it's your time to move, it's my time
C6
B♭
F
to move. Come on, come on, let go, leave it all

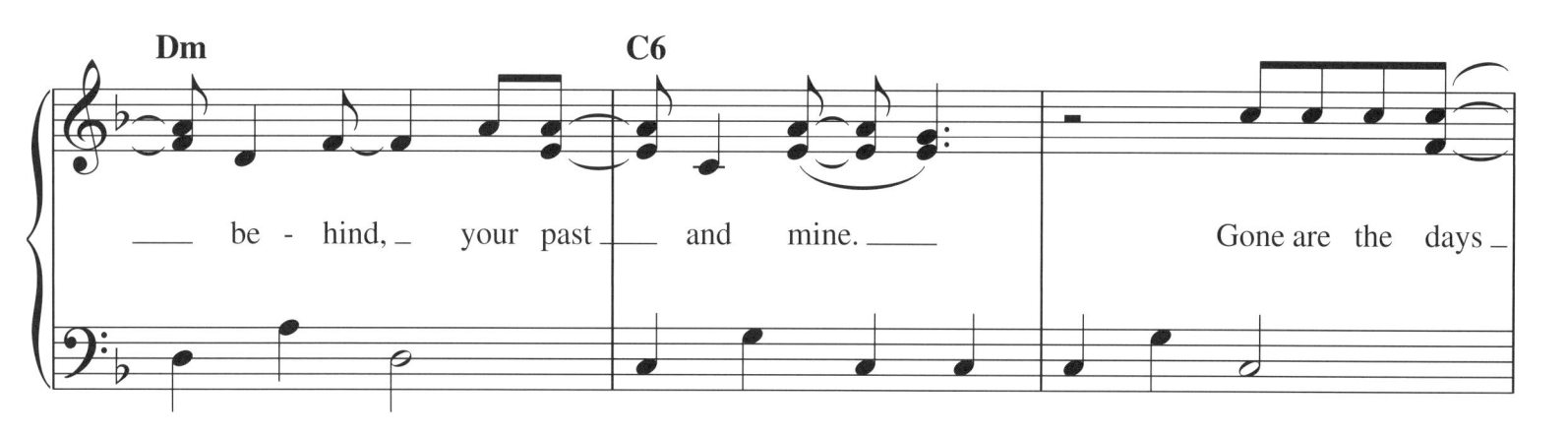

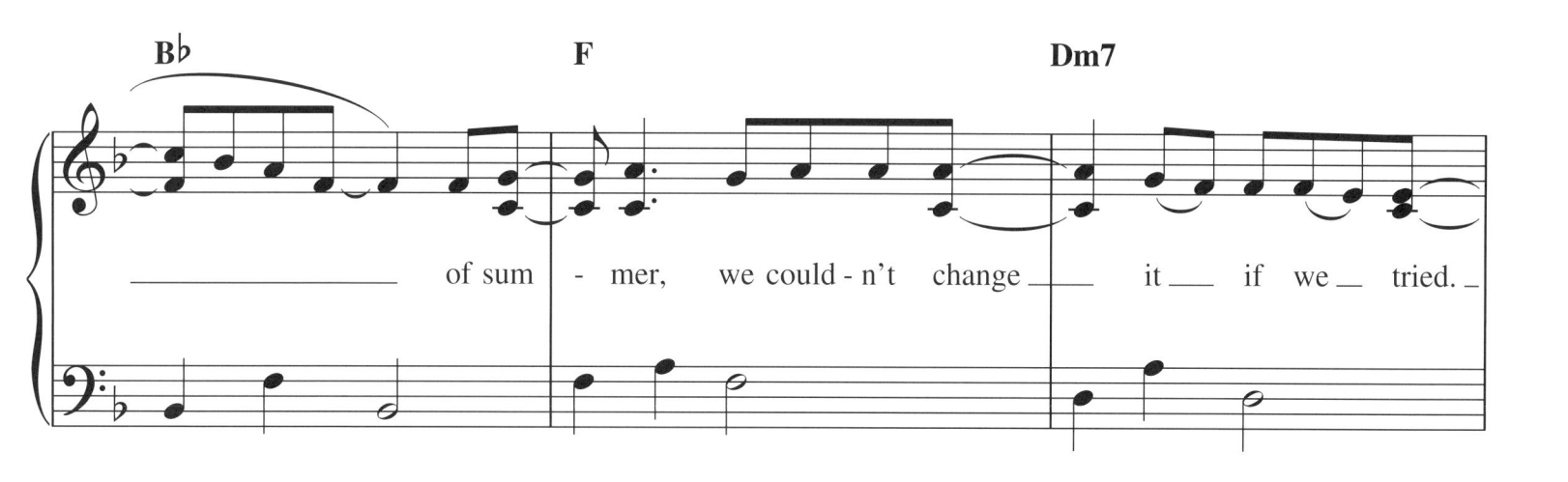

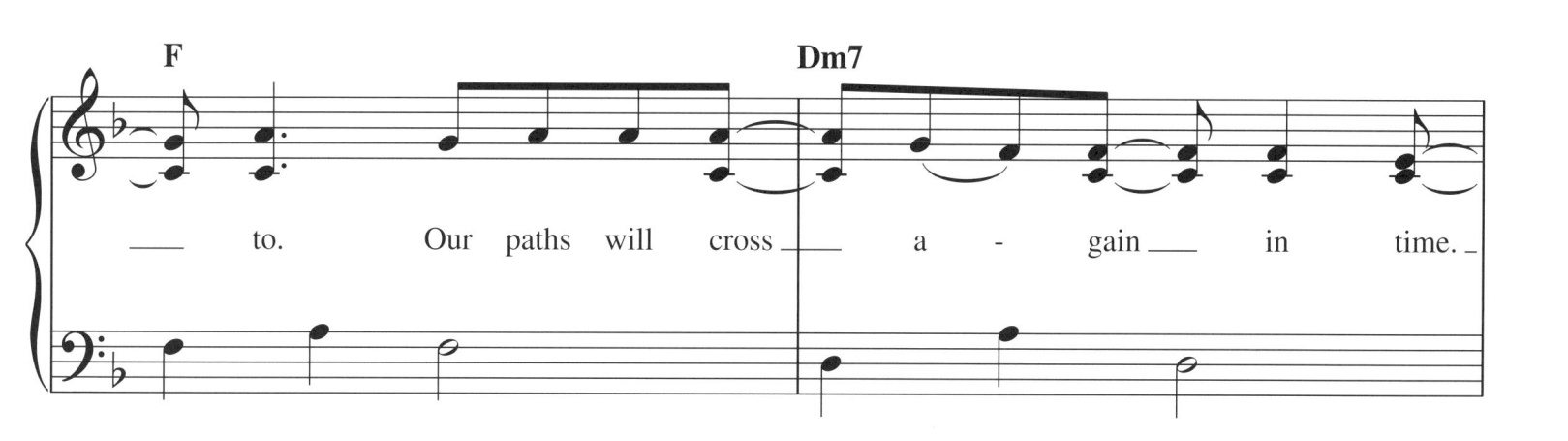

be - hind, your past and mine. Gone are the days of sum - mer, we could - n't change it if we tried. Why would we want to? Let's go where we've got to. Our paths will cross a - gain in time.

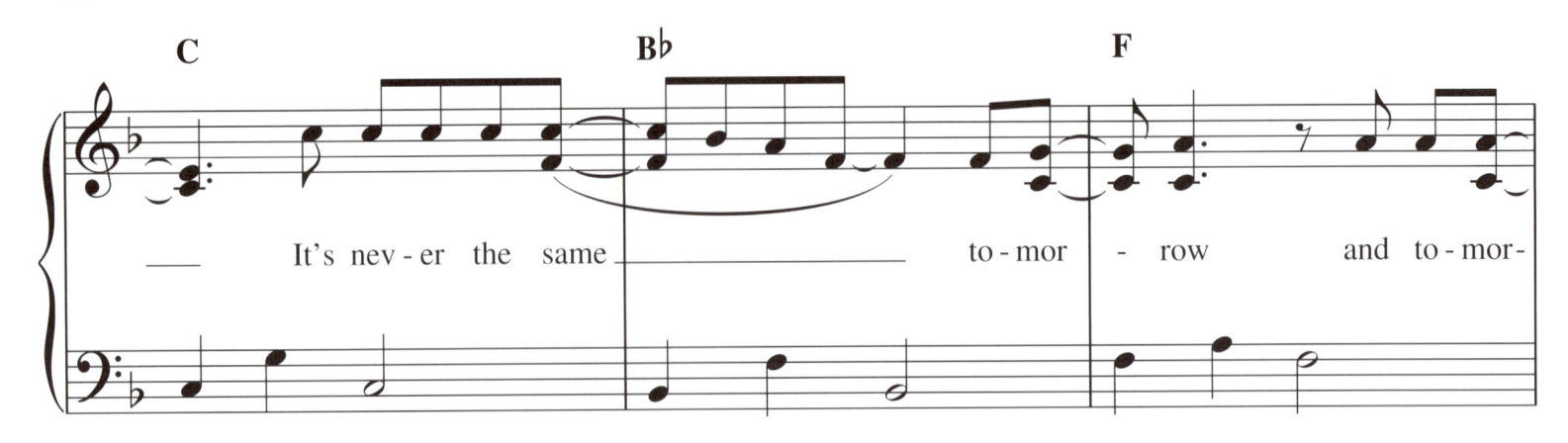

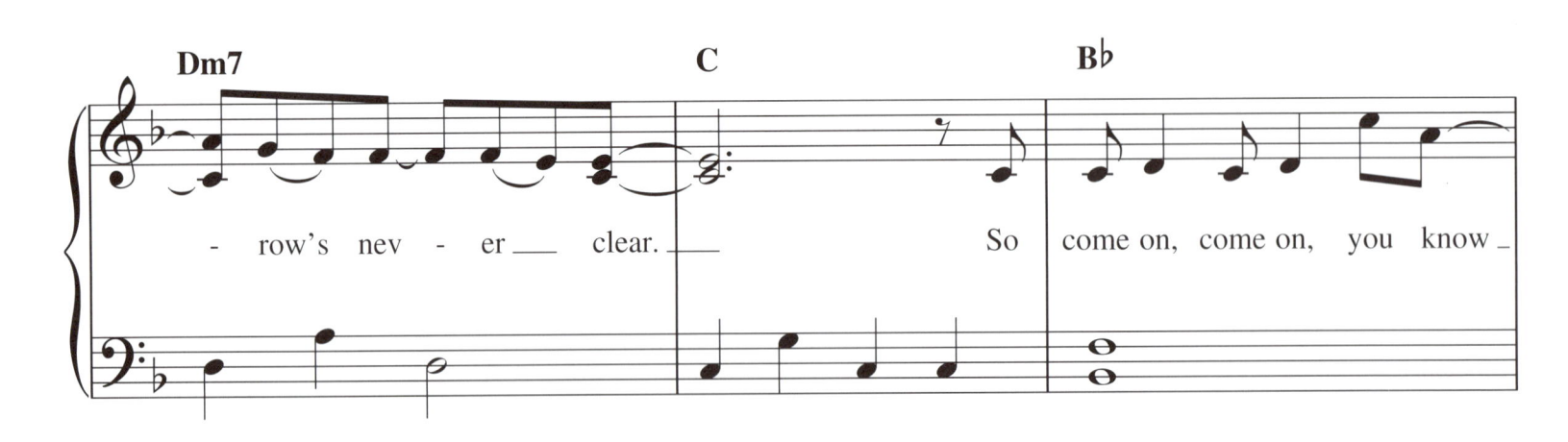

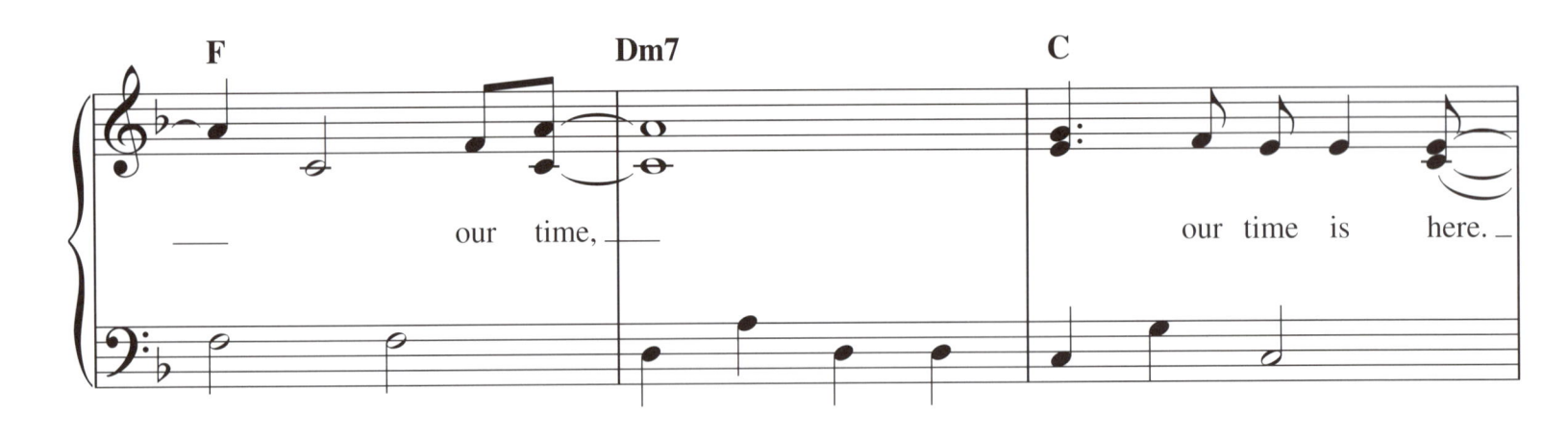

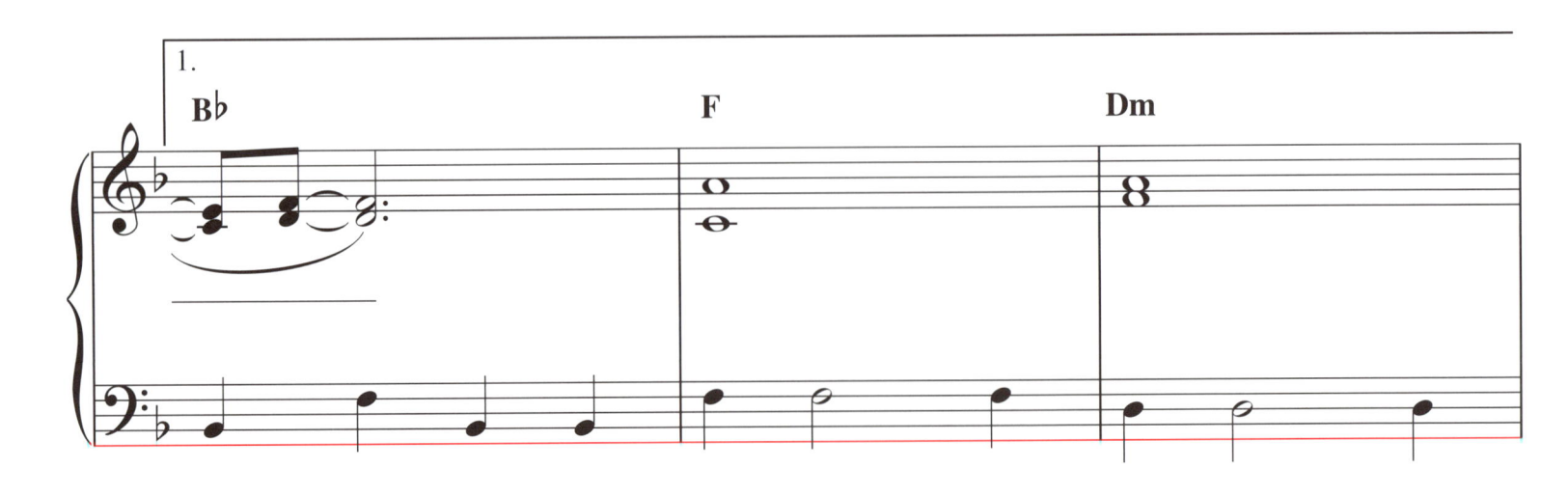

It's nev-er the same _____ to-mor - row and to-mor- -row's nev - er _____ clear. _____ So come on, come on, you know _____ our time, _____ our time is here. _____

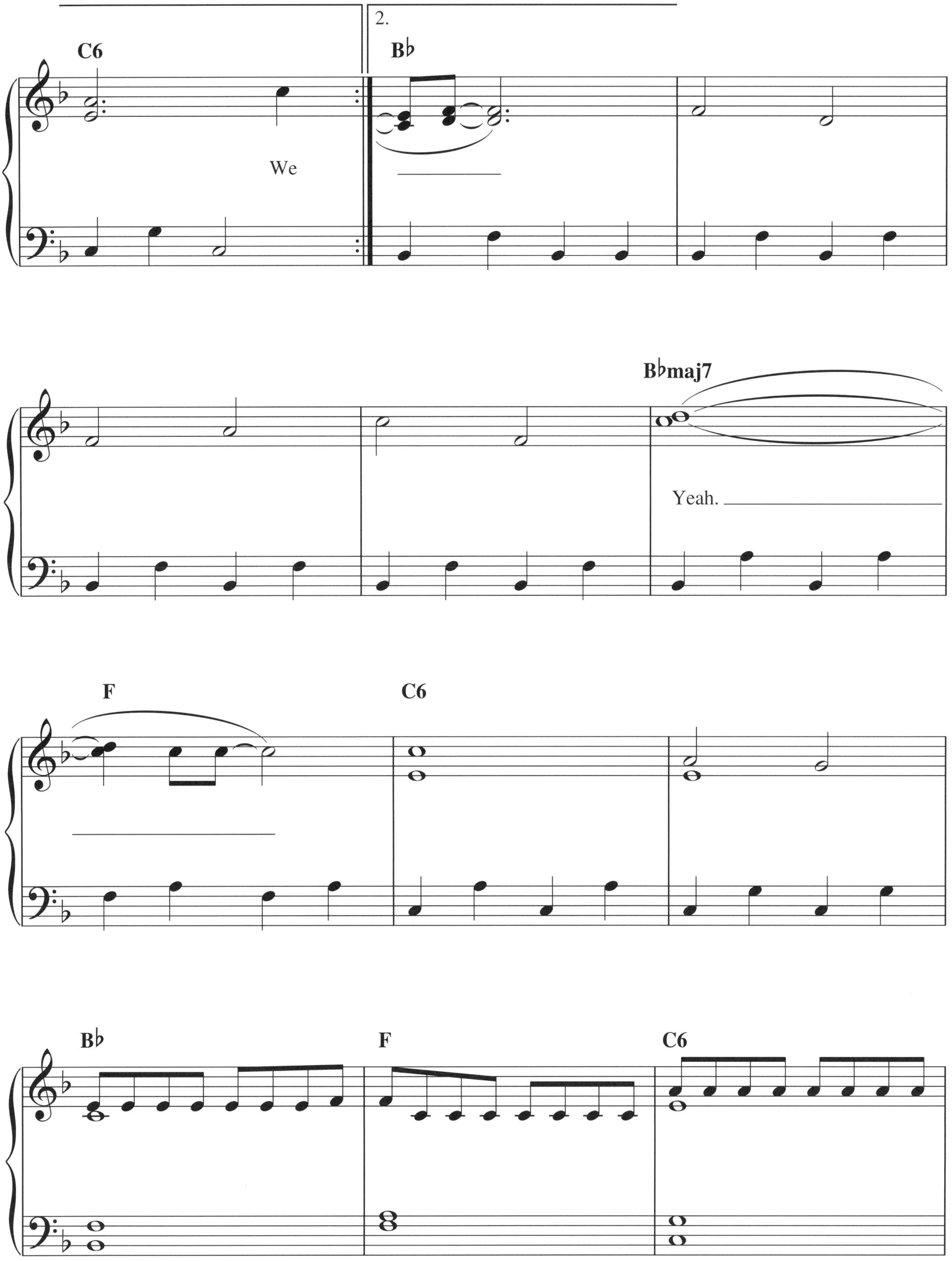
2.
C6
B♭
We
B♭maj7
Yeah.
F
C6
B♭
F
C6

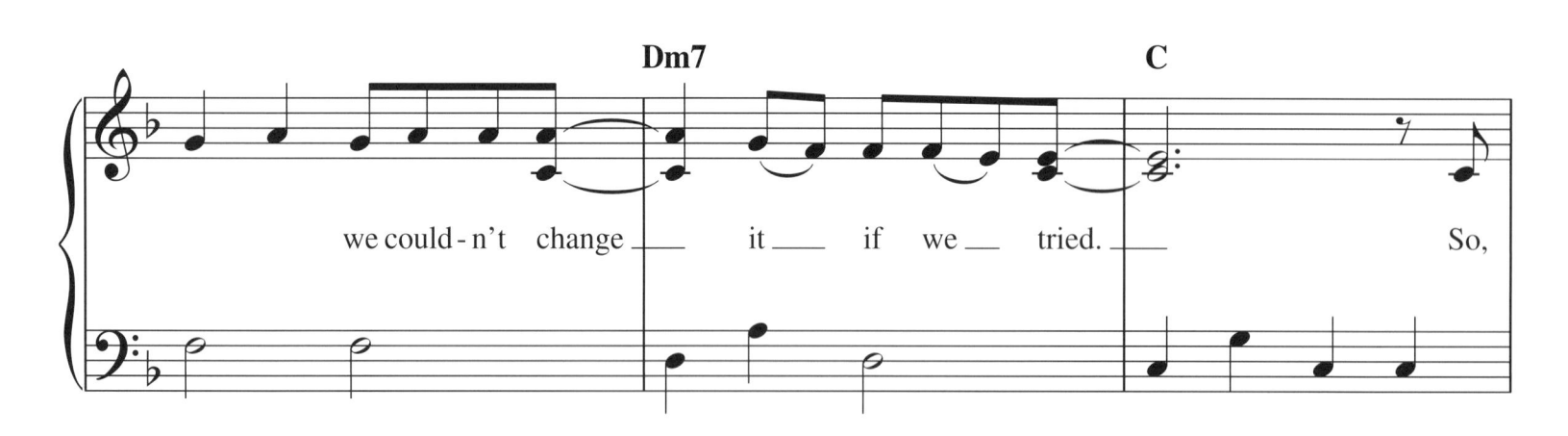

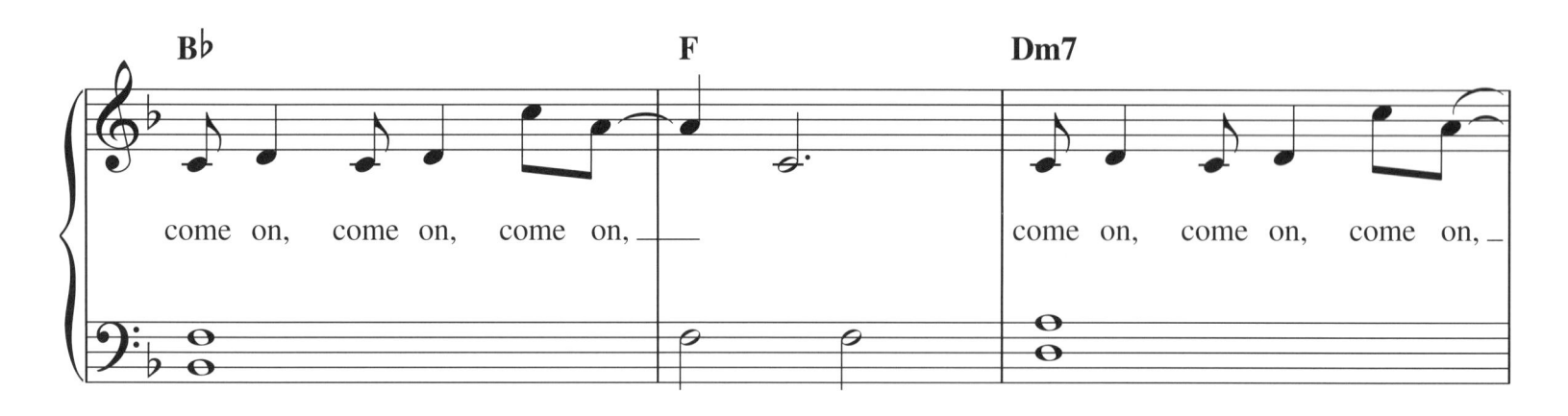

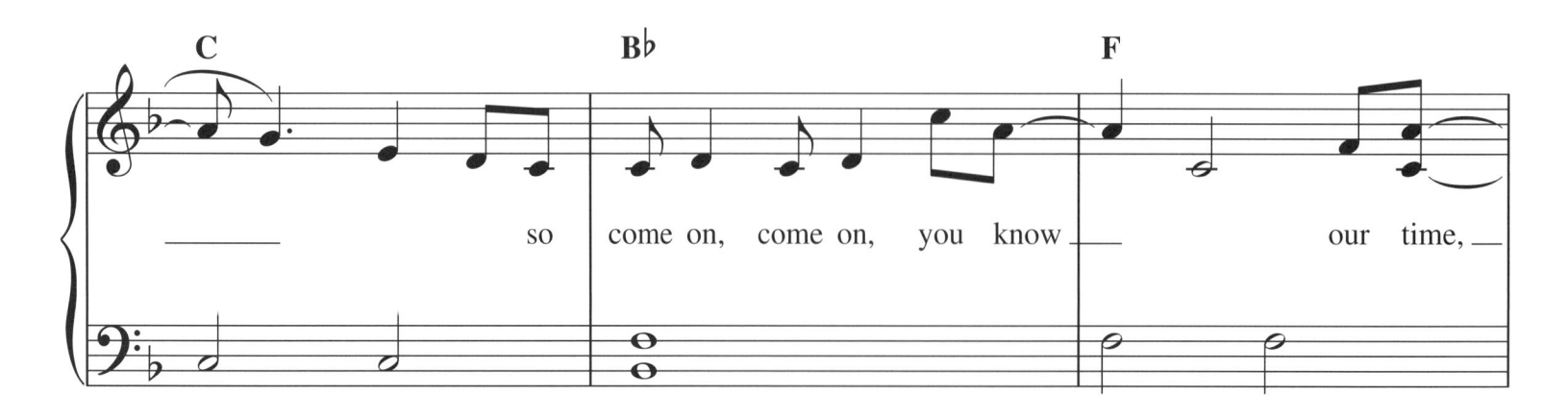

Gone are the days of sum - mer, we could-n't change it if we tried. So, come on, come on, come on, come on, come on, come on, so come on, come on, you know our time, our time is here.

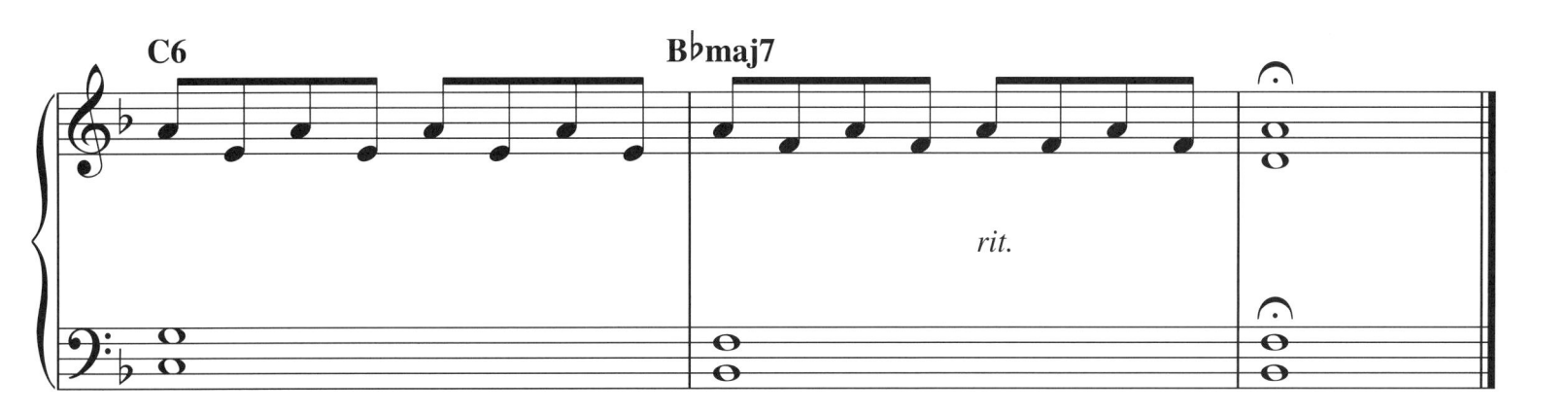

2 STARS

Words and Music by ADAM ANDERS
and NIKKI HASSMAN

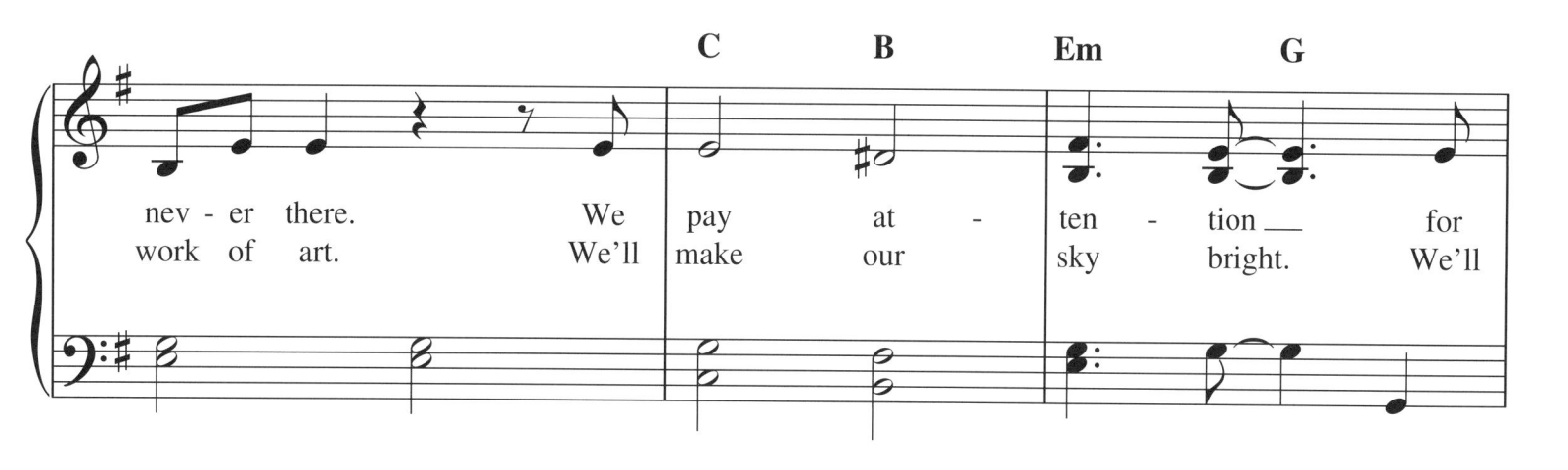

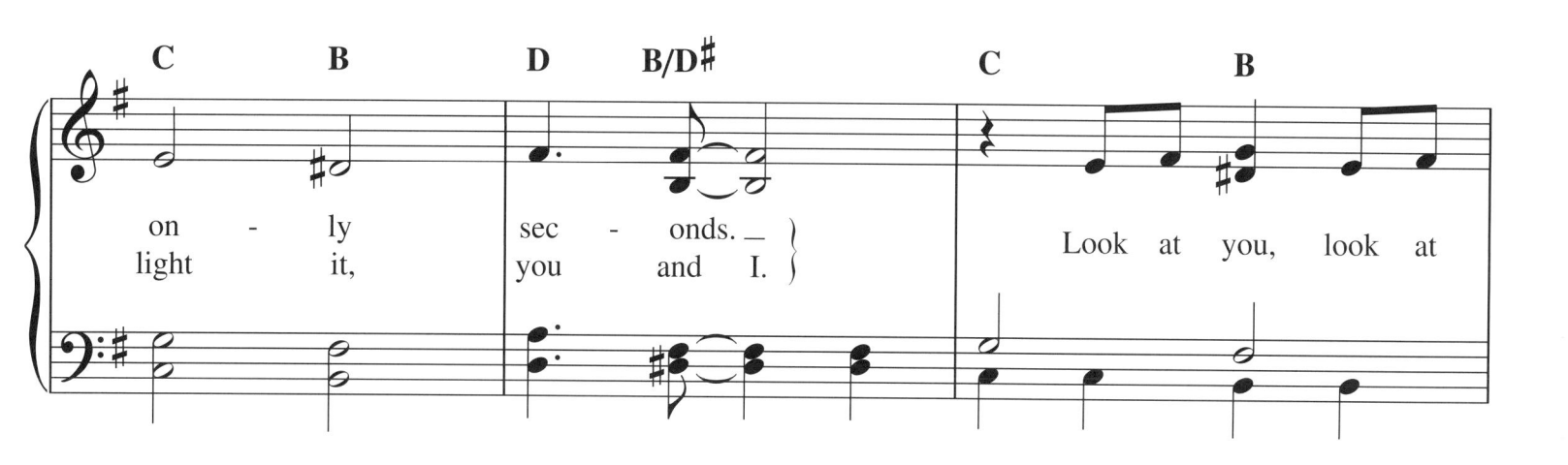

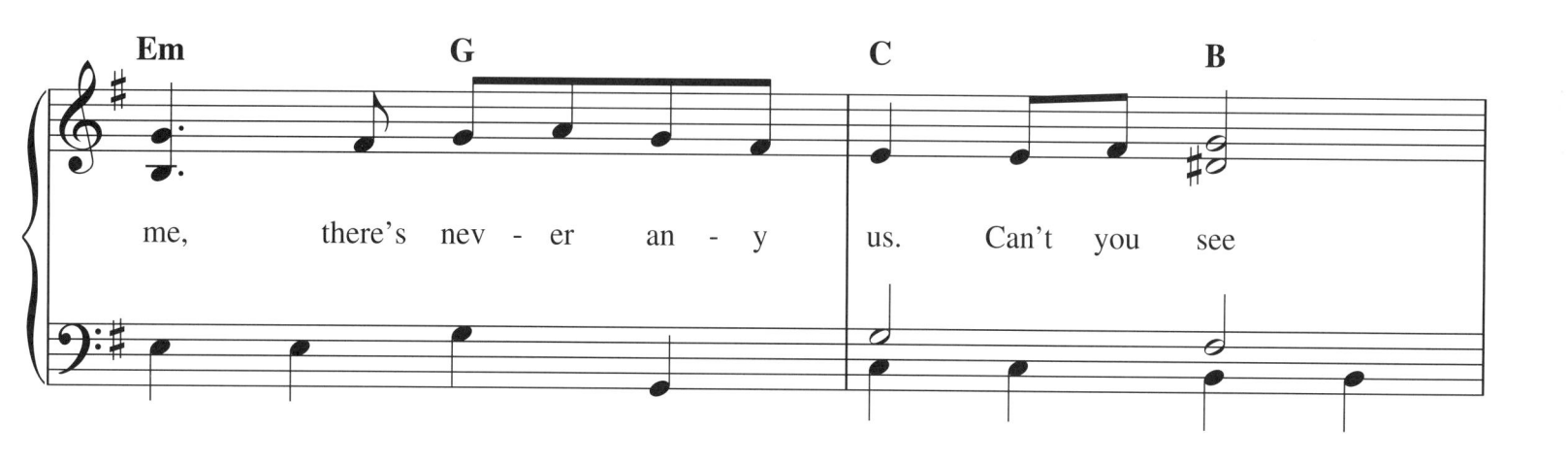

nev-er there. We pay at-ten-tion for
work of art. We'll make our sky bright. We'll

on-ly sec-onds.
light it, you and I.

Look at you, look at
me, there's nev-er an-y us. Can't you see
all we can be-come? We can shine like the

Em G C
sun if we be - lieve that two stars are
D B7/D♯ C B
bright - er than one. Come on, come on, come
Em C B
on, look at you. Come on, come on, come
1. Em 2. Em
on, look at me. on. Is it too much to ask

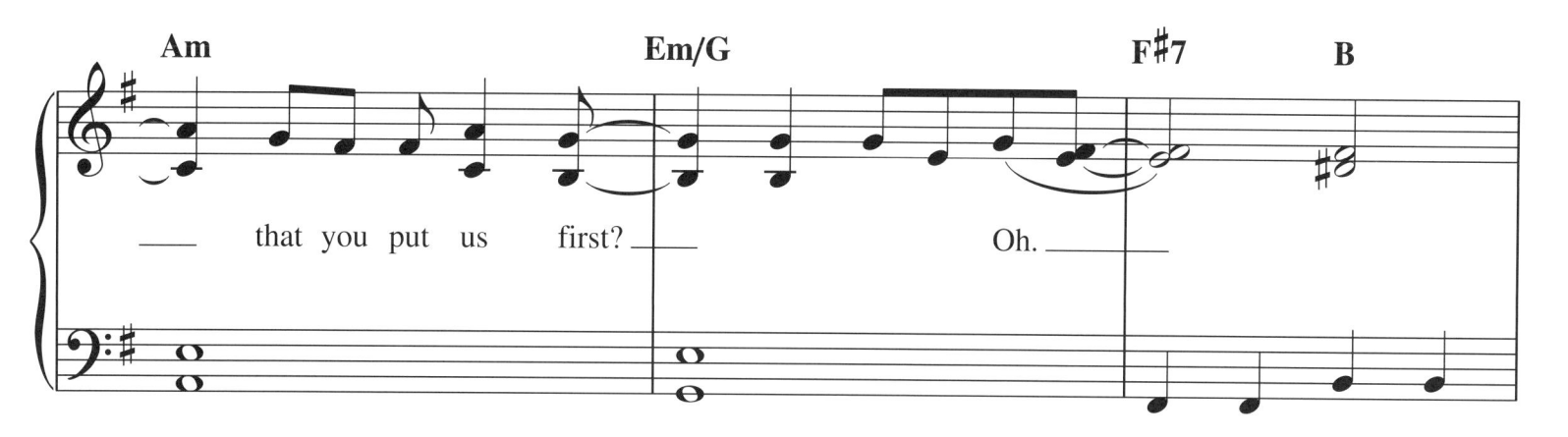

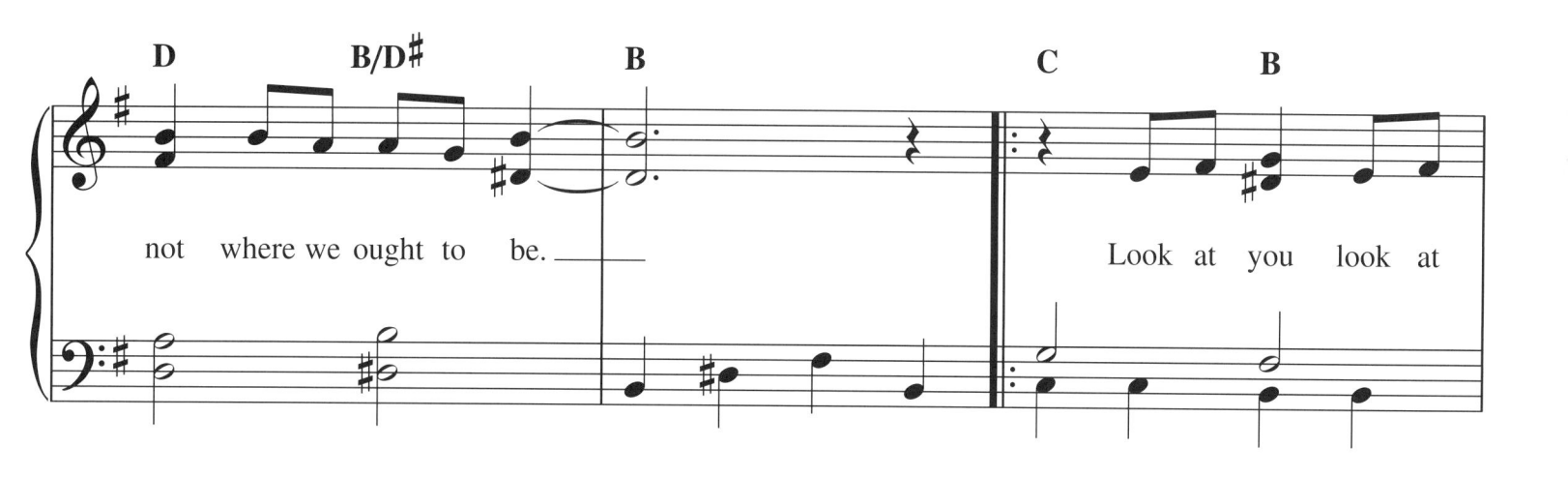

that you put us first? Oh.

I feel like we're last in our u-ni-verse and that's

not where we ought to be. Look at you look at

me, there's nev-er an-y us. Can't you see all we can be-come?

C B Em G C
We can shine like the sun if we be-lieve that two stars are
D B7/D♯ C B Em
bright - er than one. Come on, come on, come on, look at you.
C B Em C B
Come on, come on, come on, look at me. Come on, come on, come
Em C D B/D♯ Em
on, look at you. Come on, come on, come on, look at me.

WHAT IT TAKES

Words and Music by TIM JAMES
and ANTONINA ARMATO

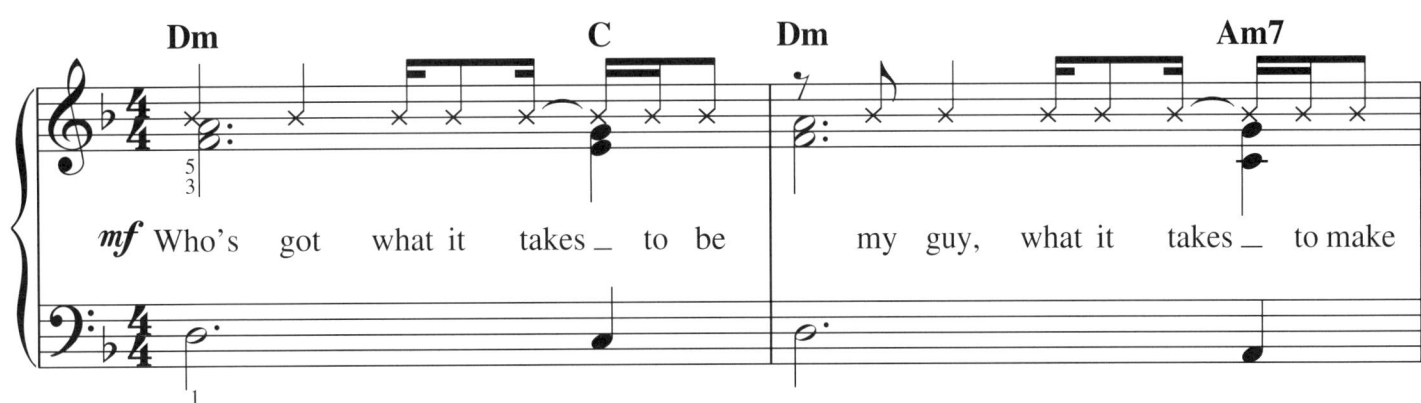

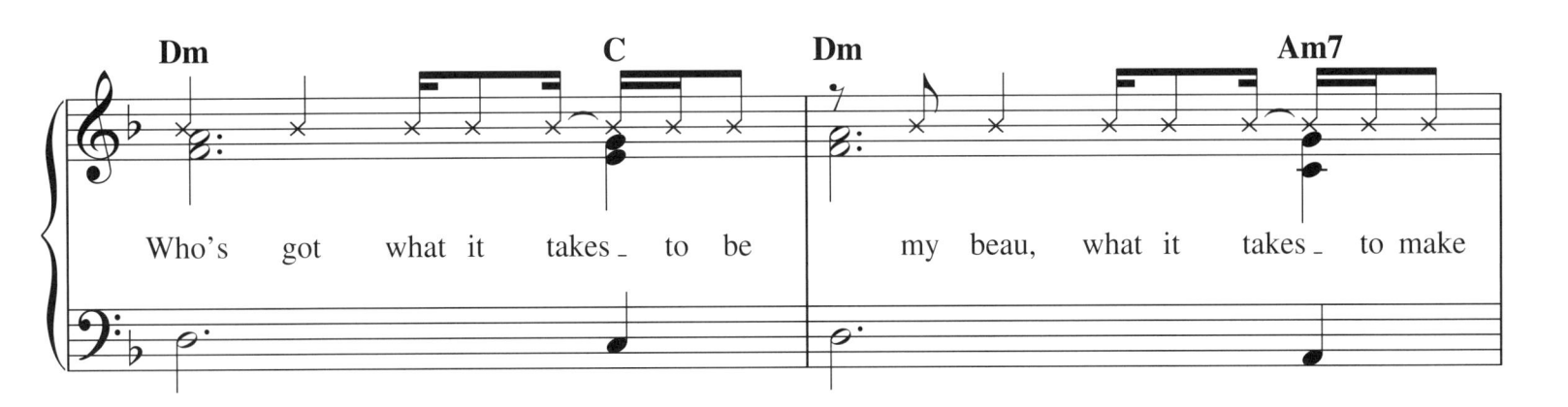

Moderate Hip-Hop groove

Who's got what it takes to be my guy, what it takes to make

me shine, what it takes to get me fired up?

Who's got what it takes to be my beau, what it takes to make

To Coda

me glow, what it takes to make this beat flow?

© 2008 Walt Disney Music Company and Wonderland Music Company, Inc.
All Rights Reserved   Used by Permission

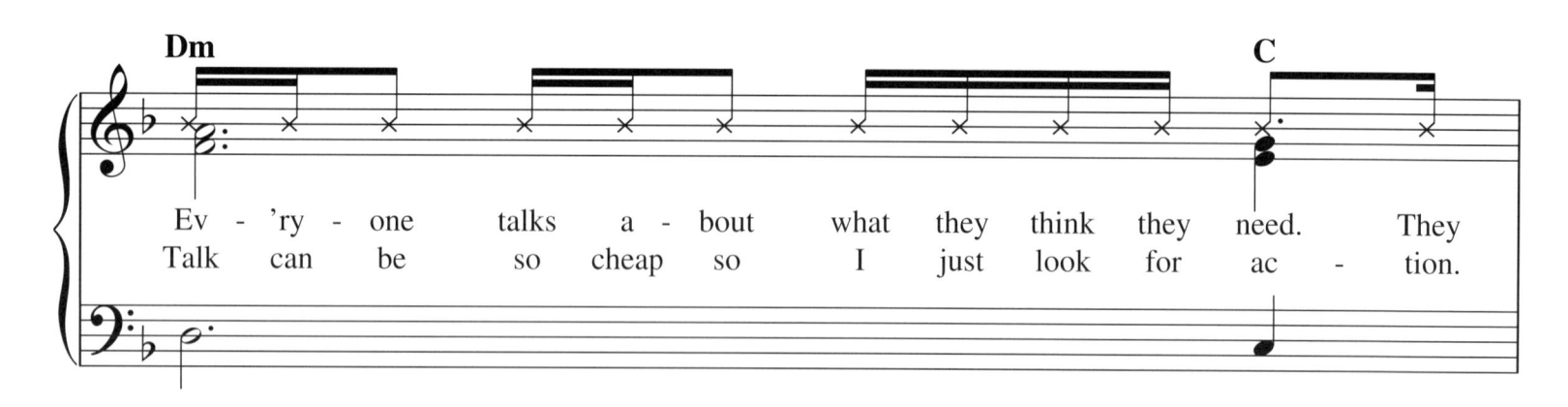

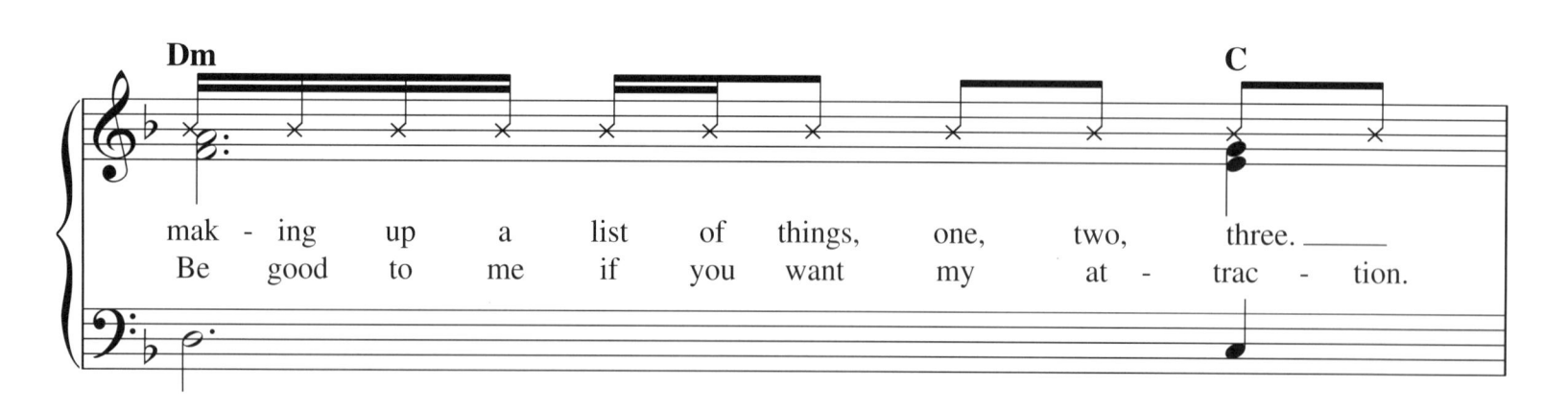

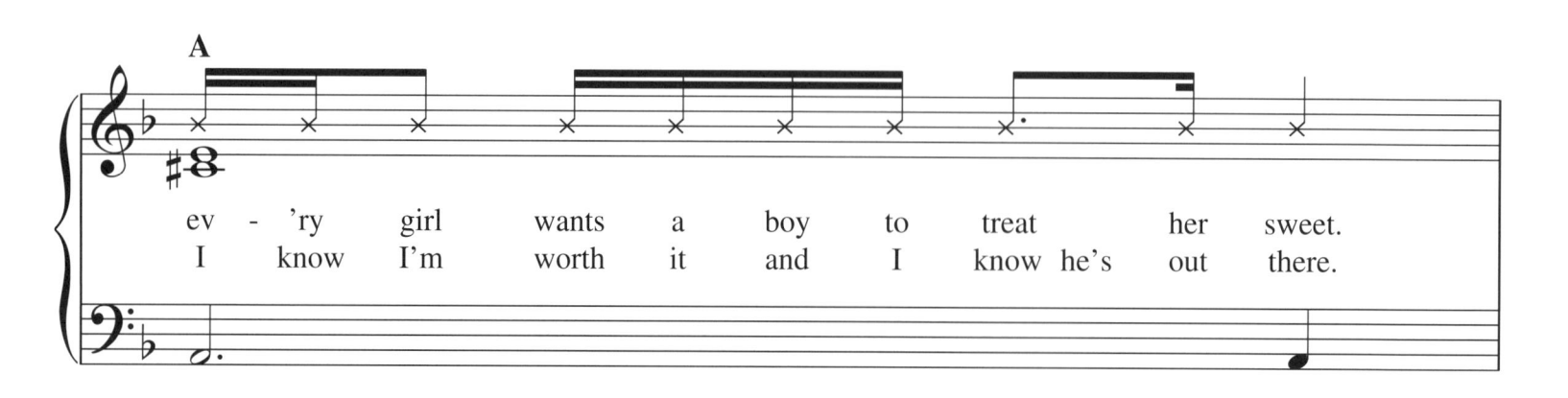

74

Dm | | | | | **C**

Ev - 'ry - one talks a - bout what they think they need. They
Talk can be so cheap so I just look for ac - tion.

Dm | | | | | **C**

mak - ing up a list of things, one, two, three.
Be good to me if you want my at - trac - tion.

G

Ev - 'ry - one is dif - f'rent but where we can a - gree:
May - be I just want too much but I don't real - ly care.

A

ev - 'ry girl wants a boy to treat her sweet.
I know I'm worth it and I know he's out there.

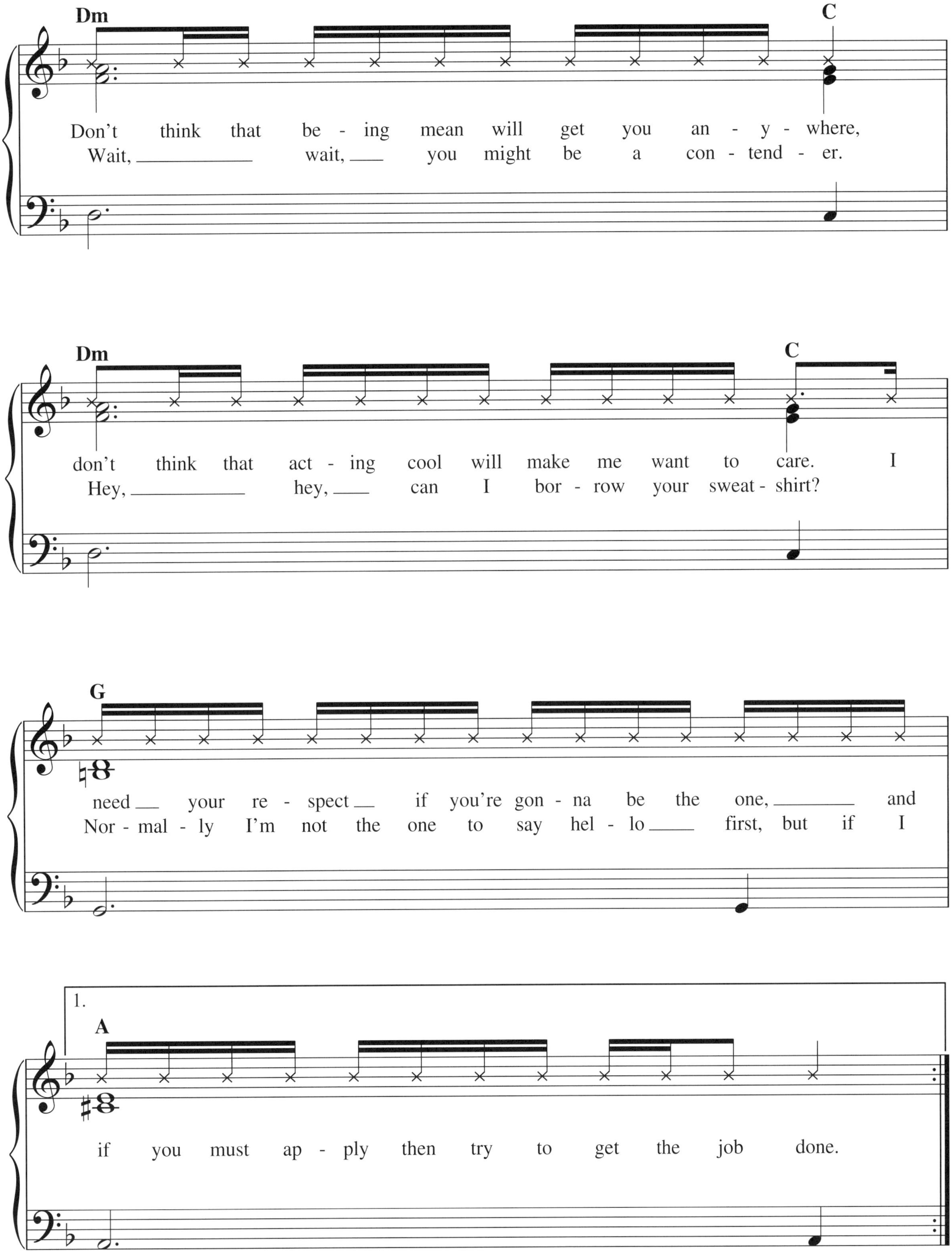
Dm
C
Don't think that be - ing mean will get you an - y - where,
Wait, wait, you might be a con - tend - er.
Dm
C
don't think that act - ing cool will make me want to care. I
Hey, hey, can I bor - row your sweat - shirt?
G
need your re - spect if you're gon - na be the one, and
Nor - mal - ly I'm not the one to say hel - lo first, but if I
1.
A
if you must ap - ply then try to get the job done.

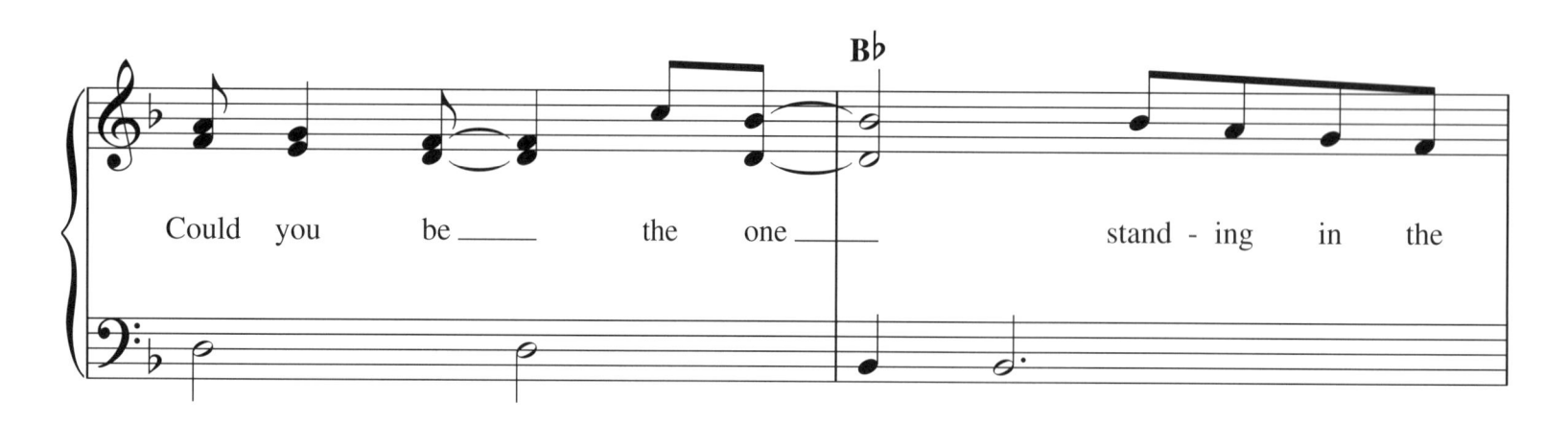

2.

A ... **D.C. al Coda**

did-n't I might miss out and that might hurt.

CODA **B♭**

I've been con-tem-plat-ing

A ... **Dm**

what it takes to make me give — my heart. —

... **B♭**

Could you be — the one — stand-ing in the

A ... **Dm**

crowd? I'm wait-ing to find — out, — I'm wait-ing, wait-ing, wait-ing, oh!

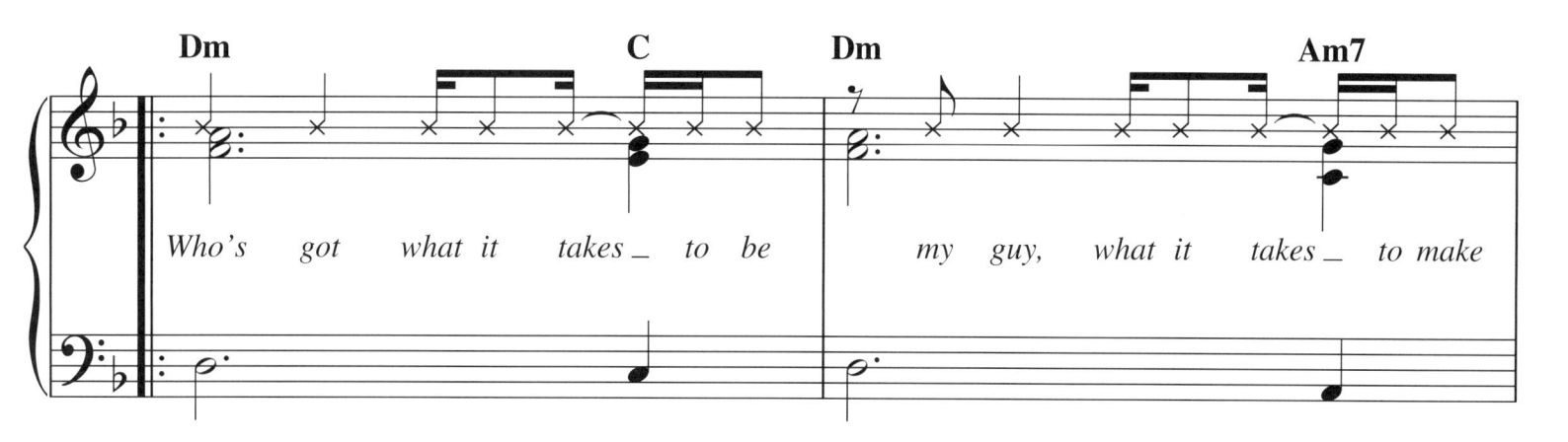

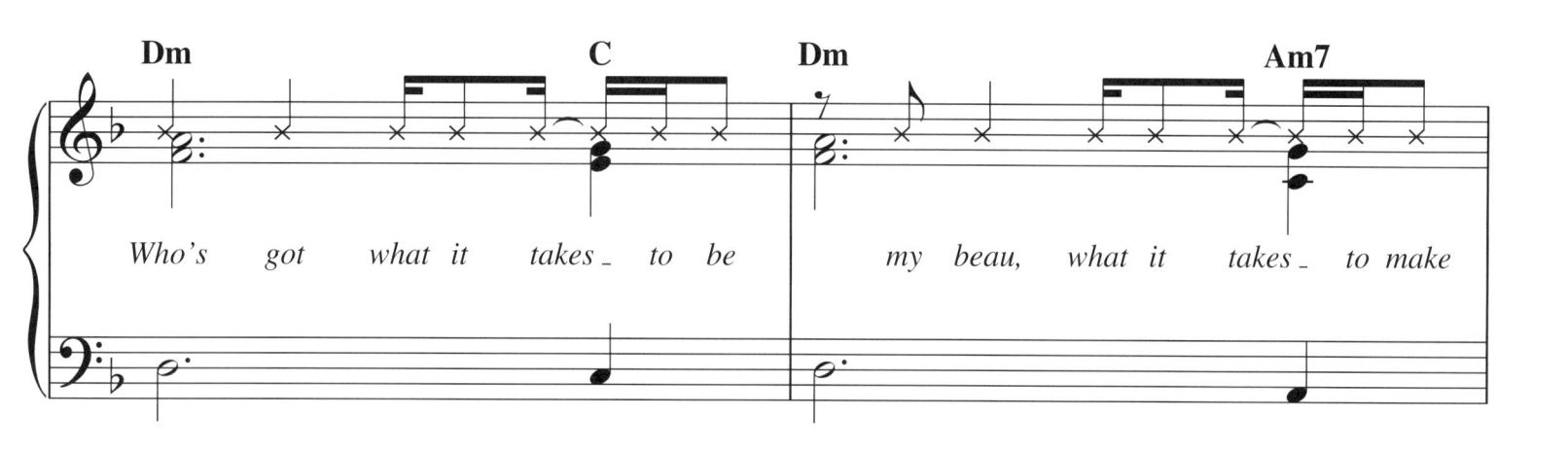

Who's got what it takes to be my guy, what it takes to make me shine, what it takes to get me fired up?

Who's got what it takes to be my beau, what it takes to make me glow, what it takes to make this beat flow?